131 FUN-damentals
for C

Liguori's Fun Facts Series

To learn more fun facts, look for these books:

365 Fun Facts for Catholic Kids

A yearful of mind-bogglers and grin-gigglers to help you
meditate and cogitate on every date. It's great! (65475)

115 Saintly Fun Facts

Holy Halo! Saintly surprises plus amazements and
amusements plus discoveries and delights. (54526)

150 Fun Facts Found in the Bible

Stories of lions and legends, heroes and heretics, and
oodles of fun facts—all found in the Bible! (54530)

130 Fun Facts From God's Wonder-Filled World

A world of fun facts about sneezes and sandcastles, bald eagles
and bullfrogs, hedgehogs and insect architects. (54528)

131 FUN-damental Facts for Catholic Kids

Liturgy, Litanies, Rituals, Rosaries, Symbols, Sacraments, and Sacred Surprises

Bernadette McCarver Snyder
Illustrated by Chris Sharp

Liguori
LIGUORI, MISSOURI

Imprimi Potest:
Thomas D. Picton, C.Ss.R.
Provincial, Denver Province
The Redemptorists

Imprimatur:
Most Reverend Robert J. Hermann, V.G.
Auxiliary Bishop of St. Louis

Published by Liguori Publications
Liguori, Missouri
www.liguori.org

Copyright 2006 by Bernadette McCarver Snyder

Library of Congress Cataloging-in-Publication Data

Snyder, Bernadette McCarver.
    131 FUN-damental facts for Catholic kids : liturgy, litanies, rituals, rosaries, symbols, sacraments, and sacred surprises / Bernadette McCarver Snyder ; illustrated by Chris Sharp.—1st ed.
        p. cm. — (Liguori's fun facts series)
    Includes index.
    ISBN 978-0-7648-1502-7
    1. Catholic Church—Miscellanea—Juvenile literature. 2. Catholic church buildings—Miscellanea—Juvenile literature. I. Title. II. Title: One hundred and thirty-one FUN-damental facts for Catholic kids. III. Series.
BX1754.5.S69 2006
282—dc22   2006016197

Liguori Publications, a nonprofit corporation, is an apostolate of the Redemptorists. To learn more about the Redemptorists, visit *Redemptorists.com*.

Printed in the United States of America
11 10 09 08   5 4 3 2

Dedication

For all the children who have questions and all the adults who are looking for answers. For all who know that questioning is the first step to knowledge but knowledge is not the last step to understanding. With humble acceptance of the fundamental fact that only God has all the answers.

Introduction

Why don't airplanes fly like birds—by flapping their wings? Why do little brown bats sleep almost twenty hours a day but tall giraffes sleep less than two hours? And what does "fundamental facts" mean?

You may have some questions that are even more interesting than those—but let's start with fun-damental facts. The word *fundamental* usually means "basic, essential, deep-rooted, the foundation of a structure." And the title, *FUN-damental Facts,* means this book will try to answer some of your questions about the basic things you might see in the structure of a Catholic church.

You might see a lion or a lily, a banner or a boat, a fish or a fountain. Just looking at the outside of a church, you might not think it could hold such things. But INSIDE…ah, so many surprises!

Just wait until you hear about monstrances and aspergillums, epistles and apostles, pulpits and pyx.

(But you won't find out about why airplanes don't have flappable wings or why bats are sleepier than giraffes. You'll have to find that out on your own.)

**Did you ever take a tour on a class field trip?
Did you ever visit a factory or a museum or a pumpkin
patch? What about a tour of a Catholic church?**

Now at first, you might think that sounds boring—just like you
MIGHT think seeing a new movie or taking a karate class or
going to the Grand Canyon sounds boring UNTIL you see, take
or go!

Anything can SOUND boring until you LEARN ABOUT
it. In this book, we'll "tour" the church inside and outside. So
come along on this adventure and the church you thought was
boring might surprise you!

Have you ever noticed that houses come in all "flavors" and colors—tall, small, red brick, gray stone, fancy, or plain. What about churches?

When you ride around town, see how many KINDS of houses AND churches you can count.

Then think about the way houses and churches are a lot alike! They are both places where babies, grandmas, teenagers, and ALL kinds of people can gather together. That's why a Church is not just the building. The people who come together to pray as the family of God can turn a building into a Church just the way a family turns a house into a home. And since you are a "child of God," a member of God's family, you are an important part of the "Church." Did you know that?

If you could build a house, what would it look like? If you could build a church, what would it look like?

What would the people who ARE the Church look like? And how would they act when they are at church OR when they are at home?

There are lots of things to see and learn about the Catholic church, but what does *catholic* mean?

The word *catholic* means "universal" or "all over the world," and there are Catholic churches all over the world. Catholic is also used to describe the members, churches, schools, laws, and clergy (priests, bishops, and so on) who follow the same teachings that Jesus gave to his apostles when he was on earth.

If you have been baptized in the Catholic church, you are called a Catholic and that's why you might like to learn all this "stuff" about YOUR church!

Did you ever dip your toe into the water of a swimming pool, lake, or river? Did you ever dip your fingers into water at church?

When you go into the door of a Catholic church you will probably see something called a **holy water font**. It may or may not look like a "fountain." It may be a large container of water on a pedestal in the middle of the floor OR a small container attached to the wall.

People dip their fingers into the water and make the Sign of the Cross. The water is not called "holy" because it's magic or anything like that, but because a priest has prayed over it and blessed it. This is to remind you that you were once baptized with water and became a Christian—and you should act reverent like a Christian while you're in church.

Did you ever dip your fingers into the holy water font at a church? Did it ever make you think about how you were once baptized with water?

If your family has a picture of the day you were baptized, ask them to show it to you. When you look at it, you might see the people who were there for your baptism—people who all love you. And every time you dip your finger into holy water, you can remember that God loves you because you are a part of HIS family.

Do you know how to make the Sign of the Cross— with or without holy water?

To make the **Sign of the Cross**, as a reminder of Jesus dying on the cross, you simply touch your fingers to your forehead, then to your chest, then to your left shoulder, then to your right shoulder. As you do this, you quietly say or think, "In the name of the Father, and of the Son, and of the Holy Spirit. Amen."

You will notice that during Mass, the priest—and the people—often make the Sign of the Cross. There are lots of other times when you could make this sign. Do you know when those times are?

Well, you can make it before you start to say a prayer in class or in a group—and at the end of the prayer. You can make it when you receive the Eucharist or at the end of Mass when you receive the priest's blessing or just anytime you want to say hello to God.

You can even do it secretly by quietly using your thumb to make a cross sign on your forehead or your chest or even in the palm of your hand (this can be called your **palm prayer**!). Can you think of some times you might want to make a secret cross sign to ask God to help you—like maybe when you're afraid of something or want to say thanks for something or are just too tired to say a long prayer?

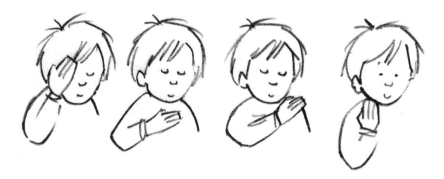

What does the Sign of the Cross have to do with the Trinity?

Trinity means "three" and the three names you use—Father, Son, and Holy Spirit—are known as the **Holy Trinity**. There's God the Father and Jesus the Son and the Holy Spirit (which is the love of God working in the world and in you!).

When you are trying to think of a new idea or a new way to solve a problem, you can ask the **Holy Spirit** to "inspire" you or wake up your brain and help you come up with the right answer. There's a Holy Spirit prayer that some people say. But YOU can just say, "Come, Holy Spirit, HELP!"

One of the first things people do when they come into church is called "genuflecting." Can you guess what that means?

OOPS! You might trip over someone who's **genuflecting** in church or someone might fall over YOU if you are genuflecting! You may have guessed that this word simply means to kneel on one knee and bow your head before you go into a church pew. So why would anyone do this?

Well, maybe you've seen a movie where there was a castle with a king and queen and knights in shining armor. In one of the scenes, you may have seen a knight come to the king's throne and go down on one knee and bow his head before the king to show him respect and honor. That's called genuflecting. And in that same way, when Catholics go into church, they often stop in the aisle—before they go into a pew—to kneel on one knee and bow their head to show respect and honor for God the Son who is present in the Holy Eucharist. Do you ever genuflect when you go into church? Don't you think that's a very good idea to do that?

**Now that you're in church, what do you see down front—
a picnic table, a dinner table, a TV table?
Noooo...noooo...of course, not!**

You see an **altar**—and it's a very special, very holy "table,"
because that's where the priest celebrates Mass. The Mass
reminds us of what happened the night before Jesus died. That's
when Jesus gathered his apostles around a "table" and gave
them bread and wine and said, "This is my body" and "This is
my blood." The next day, Jesus gave his body and blood to save
all of us, the children of God. The Mass is not only a reminder
of this past event. It is also a memorial that becomes present
everytime the Mass is celebrated. So the Mass reminds us of a
sacrifice—a sad time—and of a meal—a happy time—and even
today—when Jesus was together with his friends.

At the Mass, people come together as a "mass," a group, to
pray together in public to tell all the world that they are grateful
for Jesus' sacrifice AND to celebrate being Jesus' friends.

When you go to Mass, do you ever think about Jesus and
his friends sitting around a table the way you and your family
or friends do? What DO you think about?

Now that you know about an altar, can you guess what an altar stone is?

In the early Church, altars were always made of stone. Today they may be made of other things BUT most of them have an **altar stone**—and both the altar and the altar stone are given special blessings before they are put into a church.

The altar itself is usually about the size of a dining-room or kitchen table, but the altar stone is only about eight by ten inches—about the size of a large book—and it's inserted into the center of the altar or attached in the center underneath the altar.

The altar stone is a solid slab of stone that has four crosses carved in the top—one on each corner and one in the center. On the bottom side of the stone, there is a small space like a secret spot where you would hide something special—and that's what it's for! Inside this space, sealed up, are two **relics**—usually small bits of things that once belonged to or were touched by a saint or a fragment of the bone of a saint. Isn't that interesting?

Of course, you may never see the altar stone because it may be covered up by an altar cloth—but now you will know it's there, just like you can't SEE God but you know he is there and he loves you.

**Here's another secret about the altar stone—
it is sometimes called a "movable altar."
Can you guess why?**

Missionaries and military chaplains often take an altar stone
with them so they can place the chalice and paten on it when
they have to say Mass somewhere besides a church—like in the
middle of a jungle or on a battlefield! That's why they call it a
movable altar.

Did you know priests often say Mass in faraway places like
that?

You remember that the word *catholic* means "all over the
world," so do you guess that maybe a
Mass is being said somewhere in the world
every minute of every day? Children like
you may be going to Mass when you are
eating lunch or playing a video game—
or going to Mass too!

**Candles look great on a birthday cake—
but why are those candles on the altar?**

Way back, in the earliest days of the Church, **candles** were used to provide light since there was no electricity but also because getting together for Mass was a special occasion. Often, LOTS of candles, which represent the presence of Christ, were placed around the altar, but today you will see at least two lit candles, one on each side of the altar.

Can you think of other special occasions when you might light candles—at a campout when it gets dark, to decorate the dinner table when you have company, at Christmastime? What other candle-lighting times can you remember?

Why is there a tent in the middle of an altar?

It's not the kind of tent you might pitch in your backyard but the word *tabernacle* comes from a Latin word meaning "tent." The tabernacle in church might look like a gold case or a square box that sits in the middle of an altar, but it is like a tent because, whatever shape it is, it's like a shelter where the priest puts the consecrated hosts.

In older churches, sometimes there are two altars. The one where the priest celebrates Mass and an older altar behind it—and the older altar is where you would see the tabernacle. In some churches, the tabernacle is to the side of the altar or in a separate chapel where you can go and sit or kneel and pray privately. This is sometimes called "making a visit."

Do you ever visit a friend or an aunt or grandpa to talk about something that's been happening in your life? Would you like to "make a visit" to talk to God about something? You can do that in church or you can do that wherever you are—even in a tent!

What are those "dishes" on the altar?

You've probably noticed some things on the altar that look like a cup or goblet and a plate or bowl. The plate or bowl is called the **paten** and holds the Eucharist (the Body of Christ), which the people receive at Communion time. The cup, or goblet, is called the **chalice** and holds the wine (the Blood of Christ.) There was a time in the past when the priest used pieces of unleavened bread to consecrate. Today the Eucharist is in fact unleavened bread molded into a more convenient shape for distribution at Mass. The host is small enough to be placed on the tongue or in the hand of the person receiving Communion.

Have you received your first Communion yet? If you have, do you receive Communion often now? Do you realize what a blessing it is to receive the Body and Blood of Christ and to feel like you are one with Jesus, just the two of you together? Do you use the time after Communion to very quietly talk to Jesus and tell him your secret wishes or problems? It's a good time to do that. If you don't, why don't you try it?

Is there anything else on the altar besides the chalice and the paten?

Well, there is an **altar cloth** (like a cloth you might have on your table at Thanksgiving dinner) and the lighted candles and sometimes pretty flowers are put behind or to the side or in front of the altar. And maybe you've noticed something called the **ciborium**.

The ciborium looks like the chalice, but do you know why it's a little different? Because the ciborium has a cover or a lid. That's because after everyone has received Communion, sometimes there are hosts left over so the priest puts them in the ciborium and closes the lid on the ciborium and places it in the tabernacle to be used at a later Mass.

Did you ever notice that when the priest puts the ciborium in the tabernacle, he locks the tabernacle with a little key? That's because the hosts are very holy and must be locked up to be safe.

Do you have a special "treasure box" where you keep some of your favorite things? If you don't, wouldn't you LIKE to have one?

And wouldn't you like to have a key to lock the box and keep all your treasures safe?

Well, the tabernacle is the treasure box in church, because Jesus in the host is the greatest treasure there is!

You probably know what a sergeant is, but do you know what a corporal is?

If you know anyone in the Army—or if you play with toy soldiers—you may know that a soldier starts out as a private, gets promoted to a corporal, and then to a sergeant. But do you know what a **corporal** in church is? It isn't anything like a soldier!

This corporal is simply a small white cloth that is placed ON TOP of the altar cloth before Mass begins so that it will catch any tiny pieces of the consecrated hosts if they should fall from the chalice or paten. The word *corporal* is used because the Latin word for *body* is "corpus"—and the hosts on the altar become the corpus or "Body of Christ."

Did you ever see your mom or grandma put a placemat on top of the table or the tablecloth so it will catch anything anyone spills during dinner? Of course, YOU would never spill anything, would you—but someone might!

You probably know about toothpicks and "best picks" for a game, but do you know what a pyx is?

Did you ever notice a man or woman go up to the altar before Mass and put a little gold box on the altar? During Mass—after Communion—the priest will open the little box and put a host inside, then close it. After Mass, the man or woman will go back to the altar and take the box. That little box is called a **pyx**. That's a funny name that came from a Greek word and just means "a container to hold a host."

The person who has the pyx will take the host to the home of someone who is sick or unable to come to Mass but wants to receive Holy Communion.

If you ever know someone who is sick or cannot get to Mass, tell their family to call the rectory and ask for someone to bring Holy Communion to them. And since they may not know this word, you can tell them that the host will be coming in a little box called a pyx!

Why are so many gold things in church?

There are many Catholic churches that are very simple and plain and many that are very fancy, such as great cathedrals in Europe and America that were built many years ago. And why is that?

If you want to get a gift for someone you love very much, you want to get the BEST gift you can find, don't you? And you even want to wrap it in special wrapping paper and fancy ribbons. So even though we know God is pleased with simple love, people have always wanted to build the BEST churches they can as a special way to HONOR God. And they sometimes "wrap" the churches with beautiful architecture and paintings and stained-glass windows and decorate them with bouquets of fresh flowers and candles and golden things. It is especially important to them to have **golden** chalices and patens to hold the Eucharist.

Did you ever receive a very special present? Maybe it was wrapped in fancy paper and maybe it wasn't. But do you remember how you felt, knowing that someone loved you so much they wanted to give you the best present they could? What was your favorite present of all time?

In the summer, you've probably run through a sprinkler in the backyard, but have you ever been sprinkled with water in church?

On special occasions, the priest will walk down the aisle carrying an **aspersorium** (which looks like a fancy bucket) that is filled with holy water. Inside the aspersorium is the **aspergillum**, a long handle with a hollow round ball on the end that has holes in it. (Those fancy words come from a Latin word that simply means "to sprinkle.")

The priest dips the aspergillum into the aspersorium and then sprinkles the people with the water as a special kind of blessing to remind them of their baptism with water. If the priest doesn't have an aspergillum, he might use a green branch to dip in the holy water. This is called the "rite of sprinkling"! Isn't that a funny name?

Do you like to get a "sprinkled" blessing in church? It might not be as much fun as running through the sprinkler in the summer, but it's always nice to get a blessing.

**Speaking of holy water, did you know you can
sprinkle some in your house too?**

Many people have small holy water fonts hanging on a wall
in their homes and you could too. Many churches have little
bottles of **holy water** that you can bring home to fill the font or
you can take a small bottle (like a clean empty baby food jar) to
church and ask the priest to fill it with holy water for you—and
you can usually buy a holy water container in a religious goods
store.

Wouldn't that be nice to have holy water at home so you
could dip your finger in it every morning and make the Sign of
the Cross to say good morning to God?

**And speaking of the "rite" of sprinkling,
do you think there are other rites, writes, or rights
in church?**

There are all three! The word *rite* simply means "a religious
custom or ceremony or sacramental act, such as the Mass or
benediction, baptism, confirmation, and so on. Once you have
been baptized, you have *rights* as a member of the Church—to
receive education about the teachings of the Church, to ask the
pastor for spiritual help, and many others. But with rights come
duties, so you also have the duty to go to Mass on Sunday, to
lead a Christian life by observing the Ten Commandments, and
so forth. And as for *write*, there are many books that have been
written to help you learn more about rites, rights, and duties.

Do you or your family have any "religious" books? Do you
ever read them together? What is your favorite book about
God?

What does the "rite" of benediction have to do with a monster?

You've probably seen lots of monsters on TV or in videos, but you won't see one in church. What you might see is something that children sometimes think SOUNDS like a monster—because the proper name is **monstrance**. This a large, pretty, golden circle with a small circle in the middle like a window. Again, the name comes from a Latin word meaning "to show" and it's used to "show" the host through the "window."

After Mass or on special occasions, the priest will take a host from the tabernacle and put it in the window of the monstrance and put the monstrance in the middle of the altar. Then everyone will say some prayers and sing some songs and this is called **benediction**.

Do you ever sit in your room or maybe outside under a tree and just spend some quiet time talking OR listening to see if God is talking to you? It is a monstrously good thing to do.

There are railroad stations and bus stations, but why are those pictures on church walls called "stations"?

Maybe they are called **stations** because when you start at the first one and walk along looking at them, it's kinda like going on a train or bus trip. That's because each station pictures one "stop" on Jesus' "journey" to the crucifixion.

You might also think of the Stations of the Cross as a picture book, because each one shows a different picture of what happened to Jesus on Good Friday. One shows Jesus on trial, being sentenced to die on the cross. Another shows Jesus falling because the cross is so heavy. One pictures Jesus hanging on the cross. And the last one shows Jesus being laid in a tomb.

These are very sad pictures so sometimes people walk around, praying at each station to thank Jesus for giving his life to show people how much he loves them.

Some day when you're in church, why don't you walk around and look at the pictures in each station? Count how many stations there are and then close your eyes and see if you can remember what you saw in each picture.

**Did you ever notice a group of small candles
burning by a side altar or somewhere else in church?
Do you know why they are called vigil lights?**

When people are sick, often a friend or family member will sit
by their bedside, keeping a "vigil," praying for them, watching
over them. When a soldier is on guard duty, he must be vigilant
and watchful. In the same way, when someone has a special
intention they want to ask for—or say thank you for—they
may go up, light a candle, kneel down, say a short prayer, and
then leave. But after they have gone, the candle is still burning,
symbolically keeping a "vigil" after the person can no longer
stay to pray. And that's why they are called **vigil lights**.

This nice little custom has been in churches for many years
and may or may not be in your church today. If there are vigil
lights in YOUR church, you might like to go up and light one
sometime and say a prayer for one of your "special intentions."

Do you know what special intentions are?

During Mass, when the people are asked to mention something they would like to pray for, you might hear someone say, "For my friend who is in the hospital, let us pray to the Lord." And all the other people in church will then say, "Lord, hear our prayer." Then someone else might say, "For two **special intentions**, let us pray to the Lord." That person may think it would take too long to explain what they want to pray for so they simply call it a "special intention."

Did you ever have a special intention you would like to pray for?

For example, you might be worried because your dog threw up on the living room carpet and you are afraid your mother won't be able to get the stain out or your dad might be mad at you because you were supposed to keep the dog out of the living room. You wouldn't want to explain all that in the middle of Mass so you could just ask everyone to pray for your "special intention."

When you go to the park, do you run around, climb up and down, and shout to your friends? When you go to a movie, do you sit quietly, watch what's happening on the movie screen, and whisper if you want to ask a question? Now which of those do you think you should do in church?

A church is supposed to be a friendly place so you might look for friends and wave quietly to them, but you would NOT want to shout or talk out loud. A **church** is the place to think about God and watch what's happening so you can pray or sing when

everyone else does. But sometimes, it's hard to remember to be quiet.

Did you ever hear about a bird called a crane? They like to cackle to one another and make a lot of noise, especially when they are flying. But that's not a good idea because all that noise gets the attention of eagles who like to swoop down, grab a crane, and fly away to have a crane-burger for lunch. OWWWW!

But you know what? Some cranes are very smart. They have learned to pick up stones large enough to fill their mouths— and this reminds them not to cackle when they are in eagle territory!

Now you would not want to put stones in your mouth because you may swallow one and end up in a hospital! But you COULD take a prayer book or maybe a holy card along with you to church so you can look at it and be reminded NOT to cackle during Mass.

But what is a holy card?

It's NOT like a baseball card, but it IS about the same size and it IS a bit like a baseball card because it sometimes has a picture of a person on it. The **holy card** may have a picture of a favorite saint—like Saint Francis. And if you get squirmy during Mass, you could look at the holy card and think how Saint Francis loved the birds and animals and think about all the animals God made—and try to decide on a favorite one. OR the holy card may have a short prayer on it so you could try to memorize the prayer and say it every time you are in church—like maybe, "This is the day the Lord has made. Let us rejoice and be glad!"

If you don't have any holy cards, ask someone to help you get some!

Have you ever wondered why the priest and some other people on the altar are wearing long funny clothes instead of blue jeans?

If you ever go to a college graduation or a wedding, you will notice that some people there are wearing special clothes for a special event. The graduates wear long loose gowns and funny-looking square hats that have a tassel hanging off the side. At a wedding, the bride usually wears a long fancy white gown and veil and the groom wears a black suit called a tuxedo.

Well, Mass is a VERY special event so the priest and some of the people on the altar wear special clothes and they are called "**vestments**." Did you know that?

There are bulletproof vests police wear and life-preserver vests you wear on a boat—but what are vestments?

The word *vestment* comes from a Latin word that simply means "to clothe," but a vestment is a kind of clothing that a priest wears OVER his regular clothes when he is at the altar during Mass, a wedding, funeral, baptism, and so on. Each vestment has a special name.

The **amice** is a square or oblong piece of material with two long tapes attached that a priest sometimes wears over his shoulders to symbolize the "helmet of salvation." Then he puts on a long white garment called an **alb**, which symbolizes the purity one should be covered with when approaching God.

Next the priest wraps a **cincture,** or cord, around his waist to keep the alb in place. And he adds a long thin **stole** around his neck and shoulders (like the scarf or muffler you might wear in the winter). This symbolizes that he is "yoked" or attached to God (or maybe it's like God putting his arms around the priest's shoulders with a hug).

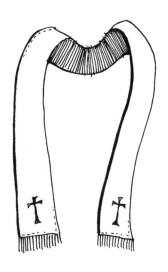

The vestment you SEE on the outside is called the **chasuble**. It's a long robe made of one piece of material with a hole in the middle so the priest can put his head through. It drapes like a cape without sleeves. And it's called a chasuble because that word comes from a Latin word which means "little house" and when the priest pulls it on over his head, it's like he's in a little house! The color of the chasuble changes with the Church seasons and can be red, violet, white, green, rose, or even black.

What's your favorite color? If it's orange, lemon-lime, or hot pink, you probably won't ever see your favorite color in a chasuble!

Speaking of a little house, do you see anything in church that reminds you of a little house—or a little room?

You've probably seen people going in there, one at a time, or even standing in line, waiting for their turn to go in. Well, that little room is called a **reconciliation room,** or **confessional**.

It's a separate place where anyone can go and talk quietly to the priest without anyone else hearing him or her. You can "confess" to God, through the priest, any sins you may have committed, even very small ones, and then ask for spiritual guidance from the priest and ask God's forgiveness.

Would you like to learn more about confession or reconciliation? Look for the listing of the seven sacraments later in this book.

While you're looking around the church, look up near the altar and see if you can spot another "table."

As you know, the altar is a very special "consecrated" table, but there is a much smaller table nearby that is called the **credence table**. It's simply a small table that usually is covered in a white cloth, and it holds all the things that will be used in the Mass—like the chalice, paten, cruets (small bottles of water or wine), and purificators.

This may sound like a funny word for a table, but you might have something similar in your home—called a credenza. A credenza is a piece of furniture that may hold extra dishes in a dining room or extra books in a family room.

Do you have a credenza in your house or did you ever see one in somebody else's house or in school or a library? Did it look like the credence table in church?

And now that you know about the chalice and paten and credence table, do you know what a purificator is?

Although it's a fancy word, you might guess it's something used to purify something—and you'd be right! The **purificator** is a small piece of linen the size of a small hand towel—and it's used to wipe the rim of the chalice clean while people are receiving the Eucharist.

Have you ever noticed that some of the people giving out Communion are holding a small towel? Well, now you know that's called a purificator. Not a prevaricator or a perambulator or an alligator or an elevator or a gladiator—but a purificator!

Can you find the purificator on this page?

And now that you know some of the things the priest uses and wears during Mass, do you know what a priest is?

A **priest** is a man who is called by God to follow him and serves the Church instead of having a different kind of "career." He goes to school at a place called a seminary where he learns all about God and the Bible and the Church and then he is blessed by a bishop at a very special ceremony called an **ordination**. He promises not to get married so he can spend all his time working for God.

Do you think you would like to spend all your time working for God? You can, you know—and you don't have to become a priest to do that. Every morning, you can just speak to God and say, "Dear God, I will try to do good things today and offer my day to you because I love you."

Does anyone besides the priest wear vestments?

Deacons wear vestments similar to the priest, except they wear the stole attached across the left shoulder instead of hanging straight down. A **deacon**, unlike a priest, may have gotten married and had a family and then decided he would also like to serve the Church. He tells his family he would like to do that and if they agree, he goes back to school to study for a while and then he is ordained as a deacon so he can assist the priest in many ways, but he cannot say Mass.

Altar servers also wear vestments, but they are different from the ones the priest wears. Have you noticed that?

Do you know what altar servers are?

Altar servers are usually boys or girls who "serve" or help the priest during Mass. They carry candles in procession, hold the book the priest reads from, and have several other duties. The vestments they wear might be a simple long white robe with a belt or they might wear a **cassock** (an ankle-length robe that is usually black) and a **surplice** (a short white loose top that goes over the cassock and is shaped sorta like a poncho). On some occasions, a man or woman may also be an altar server.

Instead of ALL the vestments, the priest sometimes wears just a black cassock and white surplice when he is administering sacraments but not saying Mass.

Would you like to be an altar server and wear a long robe or a cassock and a surplice? Can you remember all the names of the vestments or can you think of better names for the vestments?

But wait! There are some other very special people who also wear vestments. Can you think who they might be?

What about a bishop…or an archbishop? What about a cardinal? What about the pope?

Yep, they ALL wear vestments and their vestments look like the priest's except sometimes they are even fancier. One of the things they wear that a priest does NOT wear is called a **mitre** (or miter.)

Now what does that sound like? A mite is something very little, but mighty sounds like something very big! Miter rhymes with lighter or tighter, so it could be something lightweight or tight weight—but maybe not. What do you think a mitre could be?

And if you had a mitre, where would you wear it?

The word *mitre* comes from a Greek word that means "turban"—so you could guess that it would be worn on the head like a turban. But a mitre does NOT look anything like a turban. So where might you see a mitre? If you ever went to a church where you saw a bishop or if you ever saw a bishop or an archbishop or a cardinal or the pope on TV, he would be wearing vestments plus the tall, pointed HAT that is called a mitre!

This is a very unusual hat because it is made of two flaps that are shaped sorta like an arch. These flaps are attached to a headband that fits around the head but when removed, the mitre can be folded flat and put away.

Did you ever dress up like a bishop on All Saints' Day? If you did, you could probably make a mitre out of cardboard and if anyone asked what you were wearing on your head, you could answer, "What does it look like? It's a mitre, of course!"

When you see a mitre, you might also see a crosier. Do you know what that is?

A **crosier** (or crozier) is the tall staff a bishop (or archbishop) carries as he walks down the aisle of a church. The top of the crosier is curved so it looks like a shepherd's crook, since the bishop is like a "shepherd" who watches over the "flock" of people who live in the area where he lives (which is called a **diocese**—or an archdiocese).

You may not know what a shepherd's crook looks like, but you know what you can do? You can look in a fairy-tale book and find the story of Little Bo Peep who lost her sheep! Since she took care of sheep, she is often pictured with a shepherd's crook so you can see what one looks like—but the bishop's staff is much taller than hers.

**What about the pope?
He wears a mitre,
but does he carry a crosier?**

From the twelfth century until Pope John XXIII (in 1958), the popes did NOT carry a crosier, but now they DO carry a tall staff. Instead of a curved top like the shepherd's crook, the **pope's staff** has a crucifix on the top of it.

    Did you see Pope John Paul II on TV when he came to America? If you did, you probably noticed the special staff he had—with a crucifix on top.

Do you know what a crucifix is?

There are things in church that can make you feel happy—happy music and pretty flowers and smiling faces of some friends—but most Catholic churches have one thing somewhere in the church building that could make you feel sad looking at it—and it's called a **crucifix**.

This is a cross with the body of Jesus nailed to it. Although when you look at it, you probably feel bad, thinking about Jesus dying that way—but it isn't put in church to make you feel sad. The crucifix reminds you that Jesus died to save the world—but he came back to life! And that is very happy, not sad.

Have you ever watched a tree change? First it has lots of pretty green leaves on it and then, one day the leaves start to turn into other colors—gold or red or finally brown. And all the leaves fall off and the tree is standing there, all bare branches. In the winter, snow might come and frost it like a cake or leave sparkling icicles hanging from its branches like decorations on a Christmas tree. But when the snow melts, there are those sad bare branches again. UNTIL, one spring day, green leaves come again—all bright and beautiful.

That's the same way the crucifix can remind you that some days you can feel sad and lonely and think nothing can ever be happy again, but THEN gradually things change and you come back to life and feel all glad again.

The next time you are in church, look for the crucifix and tell Jesus thanks for dying for you—and also thanks for coming back to life to remind you that sad can turn to glad if you LET it happen!

Now you know the pope carries a special staff, but what else is special about the pope?

You probably know that the **pope** is very special. He is a priest and a bishop and the successor to Saint Peter as the leader of the Catholic Church. He lives in a place called the **Vatican**, which is in Rome, Italy, and he is known by many names— the Vicar of Christ, the Supreme Pontiff, the Holy Father, the Bishop of Rome, AND Papa.

Since the term *pope* is a Latin word that means "father," the pope is papa to Catholics all over the world—and all the priests, bishops, and cardinals in the world help him to take care of his large spiritual family.

But did you know that each time a new pope is chosen he gets to pick the "main" name he wants to use? Recent popes have chosen names such as Pius, John, Paul, John Paul, and Benedict—but there have been lots of names in between like Felix, Clement, Julius, and Alexander. And the first pope was Saint Peter.

What do you think would be a good name for a future pope?

You know the name of the first pope was Saint Peter, but do you know the name of the second pope?

You may be surprised to know that it was Linus. Do you know anyone else named Linus—like maybe one of the characters in a famous and popular cartoon?

Ask one of your friends or one of your parents to tell you the name of the second pope—and they probably won't know. Then you can surprise them by telling them it was Linus!

You won't see a statue of today's pope in your church, but you may see a statue of a former pope—Saint Peter or Saint Leo or Saint Gregory. But what other kind of statues will you see in a Catholic church—and why?

Most Catholic churches have some **statues** on the side altars or maybe in a side chapel or even in the churchyard. You will often see statues of Mary, Jesus' mother, or Saint Joseph, Jesus' father on earth, or some special saint.

Statues are just to remind you of someone. At a major-league ballpark, you may see a statue of a famous ballplayer like Babe Ruth or Ozzie Smith. At a park, you may see a statue of a famous president, such as George Washington or Abraham Lincoln.

If you live in St. Monica Parish, you might see a statue of Saint Monica. If you live in St. Teresa Parish, you might see a statue of Saint Teresa. If you live in a parish named after an apostle, you might see a statue of an apostle—such as Saint Mark or Saint Matthew.

When you look at a statue, it might inspire you to lead your life in a certain way, to work, to study, to pray, so that some day you might be a good ballplayer or good president—or even a saint!

Which one would you hope to be?

Do you know the difference between an epistle and an apostle?

Those two words may sound alike, but there's a big difference. An EPISTLE is a message that is written down and meant to be shared. It's like a group-letter instead of a private letter or e-mail sent to just one person. And it usually teaches a lesson.

At every Mass, there are two Bible readings and a psalm reading. On Sundays there is another reading taken from the New Testament. The first reading is taken from the Old Testament and the last reading, called the **gospel**, is taken from the New Testament. Sometimes there is another reading, after the first reading, and it's more like a letter—like maybe "Saint Paul's **Epistle** to the Corinthians." Saint Paul wrote lots of letters to teach people about God and many of them are in the Bible and are read during Mass.

Do you ever write letters or e-mails to your friends or family? Why don't you write to someone today and ask if he or she knows what an epistle is?

Now that you know what an epistle is, what is an apostle?

You probably already know that an **apostle** is the name we give to the special group of twelve men who were Jesus' best friends. So you can see there is a big difference between a letter and a friend. After Jesus died and went back to heaven, his apostles traveled all around teaching people about what Jesus taught them. Do you ever teach someone about something someone taught you—like maybe how to buckle the seat belt in the car or how to put away your toys after you finish playing with them? Then maybe you are like an apostle!

Can you think of the names of some of Jesus' apostles? Thomas, Luke, John, James...how many more can you name? Did any of them have the same name that some of YOUR friends have?

What do an epistle and an apostle have to do with a pulpit?

First of all, a pulpit is not a pit you have to pull someone out of! The word *pulpit* comes from a Latin word meaning "platform"—and pulpits have been in churches since the Middle Ages, usually placed at the front but to the side of the altar. The pulpit is high enough so the person standing there can be seen and heard (that's why it's also called the **ambo,** which is from a Greek word meaning "mountain" or "high elevation"). The pulpit has a shelf at the top where you can put a book like the *Lectionary*, which holds Scripture readings, and the *Sacramentary*, which includes the things said and done during Mass.

The reader usually stands at a lectern to read the Old Testament passage, the **epistle** and sometimes the second reading, which may have been written by an **apostle**! And the priest stands at the pulpit to read the gospel and to give a **homily**. Now that you know a pulpit has nothing to do with a pit, what do you think a homily might be—a home that is little…something that is homemade…the home of a man named Lee? No, no…none of those. What do you guess it is?

In case you are out of guesses, could there be a "foreign" explanation of a homily?

You have probably noticed that lots of church words come from a "foreign" word. Well, the word *homily* does too. It comes from a Greek word that means "conversation" or a talk made to a group of people. After reading the gospel at each Mass, the priest gives a short talk that is much more than just a conversation. It usually explains some part of the gospel he has read and it teaches a lesson about God and is always meant to help the people who are sitting in the **pews** at Mass—to help them think about God and think about how they can lead a holier life.

What do you think YOU could do to "lead a holier life"? Could you read books about God, say a prayer every morning and every night, or maybe just have a little talk with God every day so you and God can become best friends?

Did you notice the word *pew* in the last answer? Do you know what that means?

No, it is not something you say when you smell something bad! A **pew** is the bench or seat you see in churches where people can sit during Mass or during a graduation or wedding or funeral that is held in church. In addition to the pews, there are things called **kneelers** and that's a really easy name to understand since a kneeler is simply the place where you can kneel to pray!

Did you know some churches do NOT have pews or kneelers—so you have to stand during Mass? But don't you think it's really nice to have a padded place to kneel and somewhere to sit while listening to the homily?

Who do you think usually gives the homily?

A priest gives the homily, and it is usually the **pastor** or the **associate pastor** of your parish. Again, you've probably noticed that some church words sound like other words. Pastor sounds like pasture and that's where a shepherd looks after his sheep or a herdsman tends to the stock on a ranch. The word also means "leader" and that's what a pastor does for the people in his parish. He looks after the spiritual needs of his "flock," keeps them together and works to lead them to know God better and love God more.

If a **parish** is very large, in addition to the pastor, there will be a priest who is an associate pastor and he helps the pastor with his work—teaching religion classes, visiting the sick, saying Mass, and lots of other things.

Besides being a pastor, what other things do you think a priest might do—teach at a high school or college, write books about God, go to a foreign land to be a missionary or…?

As you can tell, priests do lots of work—lots of GOOD work.

Do you think you could say a little prayer every day to ask God to help his priests do their work well? That would be a very GOOD thing for YOU to do.

A pear can be a good snack and a pair of socks can keep your toes warm, but what do you think a parish is?

A **parish** can be like a small city or a large family. If you live in a little country town, there may be only one parish that you belong to. But if you live in a big bustling city, there may be lots of parishes and you belong to one of those.

You may have noticed that the state sets aside a large area of land with a school in the middle and any child who lives in that area is invited to go to that school. In the same way, a parish is a large area of land with a church in the middle and anyone who lives in that area is invited to belong to that church. Of course, everyone is invited to go to any Catholic church anywhere but when you live in a certain area, you BELONG to that one parish.

The people in the parish, like in a big family, go to the parish church to pray together but they sometimes get together to do other things too—like maybe have a parish carnival in the summer or a Santa Claus breakfast in the winter. The parish sometimes has spaghetti dinners or chicken dinners (and you might eat a pear in the salad they serve!). The parish sometimes has ball fields and a ball team (and if you join a team you might wear a uniform and put on a pair of matching socks!). Do you ever go to some of your parish get-togethers? What is your favorite one?

Why do people in a parish need a missal or a missalette?

A **missal** is a book that contains all that is said or sung at Mass during an entire year. A **missalette** is a smaller book that has all that is said or sung for three months. Since the readings and some of the prayers at Mass change every day, depending on the seasons, some people like to have their own missals to use all year. But the missalette is easier to hold and read so most churches put missalettes in a rack on the back of the pews for people to use every time they come to Mass. At the end of three months, when it's time for a new missalette, the ushers gather up the old ones and put out new ones.

During the homily, the people are supposed to listen, but before and after the homily, they can use the missalettes and hymnals to pray along with the priest and sing along with the choir.

Have you noticed people doing that? If you know how to read, you can use the missalette and hymnal—and if you don't, you can just listen and enjoy the sweet sounds of prayers and music.

So do you know what ushers and hymnals are?

An **usher** is like a "doorkeeper" at a movie or a theater. The usher takes your ticket and tells you which way to go to find the movie you want to see. If you go to a theater, for a play or a concert, the usher will look at the number on your ticket and show you which seat to sit in.

Well, you never have to have a ticket to get into church. You're always welcome there. But at Sunday Masses, there are usually ushers. They are men or women of the parish who volunteer to do this job each week. They may stand at the door and pass out church bulletins or, if the church is very crowded, they will help you find a seat. They take up the collection. And, if there are visitors, they will answer any questions the visitors have about the church.

Hymn is the word for a sacred song so the **hymnal** is simply a book that has lots of hymns or church songs in it to help the people sing along with the choir. The hymnal has songs for special times of the year, like Christmas and Easter, plus songs that can be sung any time of the year.

Did you ever go to a place where you had to pay money to get a ticket before you can go in? Like maybe a circus or a museum or a zoo or a ballpark? Aren't you glad you don't have to have a ticket to get into church?

If exploratory means exploring and preparatory means preparing and explanatory means explaining, what does offertory mean?

You're right. It means offering. At one part of the Mass, you may see the ushers passing around baskets to take up a collection (sometimes those baskets have very loooong handles so they can pass them across where people can reach). The people in the pews put money or envelopes with money in them into the baskets.

This is the **offertory** of the Mass, when people offer a gift to God by sharing some of the money they have made by working. God doesn't need money but his church does. The pastor of the church has to pay to keep the church warm in winter and cool in summer, to keep the lights burning, to pay the teachers or the secretaries who work for the church, and to give food or money to the poor who come to the church asking for help.

When you and your family go to a wedding or to someone's house for a party, don't you sometimes take along a gift? The next time someone gives YOU a gift of money, why don't you save a part of it so that when you go to church, you can give a gift to God by putting some of YOUR money in the basket when they take up the offertory collection?

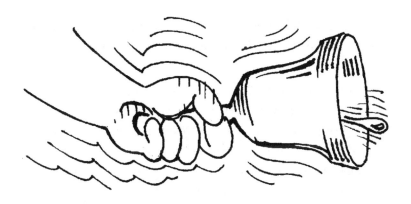

**When you hear the front doorbell ring,
you think it might be a friend...when you hear bells
coming down the street, you think it might be
an ice-cream truck...when you hear bells in church,
what do you think?**

Just before the important part of the Mass known as the
consecration, an altar server will ring some **bells**—to remind
you to pay attention to this special moment.

Have you ever noticed some little bells ringing in the
middle of the Mass? If you were an altar server, you might get
to ring the bells. Would you like that?

You may know that lava is hot molten rock that pours out of a volcano, but do you know what a lavabo is?

Lavabo simply means the "washing of your hands." And at Mass, that's when the altar server pours water over the priest's fingertips (from a cruet) and then gives him a small cloth (a purificator) to wipe his hands dry. It may seem strange to see a priest washing his hands in the middle of Mass, but it is a tradition that began many years ago when, at the offertory, for their gift to the church, people who had no money to offer brought up vegetables they had grown or even small animals like chickens.

Since the priest's hands might get soiled handling such gifts, it might have been necessary then for him to wash his hands before he began the consecration of the bread and wine. Today the lavabo is only a ceremonial washing—a symbol, a sign of the need to be purified before the consecration of the bread and wine.

Do you always wash your hands before a meal or before you get cleaned up to come to Mass? Well, that's a very good idea. You should always remember to do that!

Why is there a red traffic light in church?

Well, it's not really a traffic light, but it IS red and it should make you STOP—and maybe look and listen! It's called the **sanctuary lamp** and it looks like a tall red glass with a candle burning in it. This "red light" is usually near the altar and when it's burning, it means that Jesus, in the holy Eucharist, is in the tabernacle waiting for you to say a little hello or a little prayer of thanks, please, or sorry.

The next time you are in a church, scout around and see if you can find where the sanctuary lamp is burning. Do you think you can find it?

Here's a clue: the sanctuary lamp just might be in the sanctuary—but where is that?

The **sanctuary** is the part of the church where the altar is, the part of the church where Mass is usually said, the part of the church where sacraments are celebrated—like baptisms and marriages. The word *sanctus* means "holy" and the sanctuary is a holy area, so it is often raised a little higher than the rest of the church, with one or more steps leading to it—but not always.

Are there steps in YOUR church leading to the sanctuary? Are there steps leading into your church? Have you ever counted them?

Why don't you count all the steps outside AND inside your church?

These are all special steps— because they lead you closer to God!

_____

_____

_____

So now you know where the sanctuary is— but where is the sacristy?

The **sacristy** is a room you cannot see when you're sitting in a pew. You might never go in it or you might go in it a lot if you become an altar server. The sacristy is near the sanctuary—behind or to the side of it—or sometimes near the main entrance to the church. It has chests of drawers and cabinets and closets in it just like you have at home. That's because the sacristy is where all the "sacred things" are stored that will be used during Mass or other liturgical celebrations. It's also where all the vestments are stored and where the priests, altar servers, and so on, come to put on vestments before Mass.

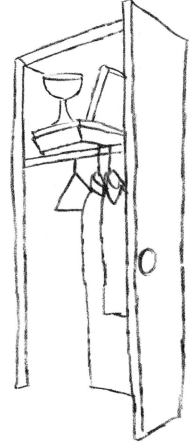

In a way, this room is like the locker room at a football stadium where the football players put on their uniforms before they come out to play the game. You can't see it if you're sitting in the stands waiting for the game to start—but you know it's there. And some day, if you become a professional football player, you will go inside.

But there is a BIG difference. No one can go in a professional locker room without a special pass, but any time you want to talk to the priest, you can go in the sacristy very quietly and ask to speak to him. And someday, if you become an altar server OR a priest, you might spend a lot of time in the sacristy.

One thing that might be stored in the sacristy and might be used in the sanctuary is called a prie-dieu—another funny word for you to learn!

This one sounds like "pray do!"—and that's just what it's for. This is a "kneeling bench" with a raised shelf so you can kneel on it and rest your elbows or a book on the shelf.

In the past, you might have seen these in people's homes so they would have somewhere to kneel to say morning or evening prayers. You just might even see a **prie-dieu** in someone's home today.

And you will probably see some in the sanctuary for special liturgical celebrations when "extra" people are on the altar who need somewhere to kneel—like at a wedding. The bride and groom often kneel right in the front of the altar during the wedding and if you look closely, you will see that they are each kneeling on a prie-dieu.

It might be nice to have a prie-dieu in your room to remind you to pray, do! But you don't really need one since you can talk to God anytime, anywhere, without kneeling down, without being in church—and without a prie-dieu!

But wait a minute. Did you notice that word *liturgical*? Do you know what that means?

There are **liturgical** books, liturgical art, liturgical music, liturgical laws, and so forth. And they are important parts of the **liturgy**. So what is the liturgy? It is the Church's public worship, all the rites and ceremonies, all the celebrations of the seven sacraments, especially the Eucharist—all the ways the people of the Church worship God. The liturgy is not just for the pope and the priests who lead the rites and the ceremonies. It is ALL of the people honoring and loving God together. And YOU are one of those people!

Aren't you glad you are?

If you see puffs of smoke in church, you might not want to call the fire department. Do you know why?

On some special occasions in church—like during processions or benediction—you will see puffs of smoke coming from something called the **thurible** or **censer**. This is a metal container that is sometimes bronze or brass and it hangs from chains. There is a small container called a boat (maybe because it looks like a gravy boat? Or maybe not.) and it holds something called **incense**. The priest spoons incense from the boat into the thurible and burns it.

The thurifer (the one holding the thurible of course!) swings the thurible back and forth so that puffs of smoke come out of it. The incense is made from powdered spices or plants that make a sweet-smelling odor when burned and these fragrant clouds of smoke symbolize prayers rising up to heaven.

Did you ever sit around a campfire and watch the smoke rising up toward the sky? Did you ever ride down a street and see smoke curling up out of house chimneys?

Isn't it a nice idea to think of puffs of smoke coming out of a censer like fragrant clouds of prayers rising up to heaven?

Have you noticed that there are a lot of interesting church words—like thurible, aspergillum, monstrance, and ciborium? If you think these are unusual, there are some even longer!

How about **Ambrosian hymnography**? That just means hymns written BY Saint Ambrose or hymns written in the style of Saint Ambrose. How about **ferraiolone**? That's just the name of a silk cape sometimes worn by a bishop or cardinal. How about **Quinquagesima**? That simply means the Sunday before Ash Wednesday, the fiftieth day before Easter.

When you want to surprise some of your friends, you can use these words—and tell them what they mean. It will be like having your own mysterious private language!

There are easy words like cat, catalog, and caterpillar, but what does the word *catechesis* mean?

This is another word that comes from a Greek word and it means "to echo." In the Bible, Saint Luke used the word **catechesis** to talk about echoing, passing on, telling others about all the teachings learned from Jesus. Today, there is another word, **catechist**, which is the name for anyone (priest, deacon, sister or layperson) who teaches children or adults the basic teachings of the Bible, the Church, the liturgy, and tradition.

Of course, catechesis can go on all during your life. No matter how old you get, you can always learn something new about God and his Church and his teachings.

Would you like to be a teacher some day? Did you know that just by being a good person and acting like you think God would want you to act you can BE a teacher? You can TELL people about God by the way you act. If you act as Jesus taught, they can learn from your example what a Christian believes. In that way, you can be a teacher!

There's a catfish and a catastrophe and a catter-corner, but what is a catechism?

You've probably guessed that a **catechism** is a book that a catechist uses to teach catechetics or catechesis. A catechism is made like a schoolbook with questions and answers. An old catechism once asked the question, "Why did God make you?" The answer in the catechism was, "God made me to know him, love him, and serve him in this world—and to be happy with him forever in the next." That's a very short answer to a very big question—but a good answer. If someone asked you the question, "Why did God make me?" what would YOUR answer be?

Did you know some teachers are called Sisters or Brothers?

Now you may have a sister or a brother in your family, but a **Sister** or a **Brother** is the name for women or men who are not priests but have decided to spend their lives working for God. They join something called a **religious order** and, like priests, they study and pray and take vows promising not to get married and to give their lives to God. There are orders such as the Franciscans, Dominicans, Benedictines, Redemptorists, and many others. Sisters or Brothers may work by becoming teachers, but they also work as nurses, school principals, lawyers, writers, or do whatever kind of work their "order" needs them to do.

Some of them take a new name—like Sister Mary Clare or Brother Andrew and people often call them just Sister or Brother, in the same way we can call any priest just by the name Father.

Do you know a Sister or Brother? Do you have a sister or brother in your family or maybe a really good friend who IS almost LIKE a sister or brother? It's good to have friends and sisters and brothers to have fun together or maybe to pray together.

Say a little prayer today to thank God for giving the world sisters and brothers and Sisters and Brothers— and friends too!

Do Sisters and Brothers wear special clothes like priests?

Well, some do and some don't. Some wear regular clothes all the time and some choose to wear special clothes all the time. And some wear special clothes for religious occasions sometimes and regular clothes at other times—the way ballplayers wear uniforms when they are playing ball but regular clothes when they are not.

The special clothing Sisters and Brothers sometimes wear are called **habits**. Different religious orders or communities wear different kinds of habits. They may be long white or brown robes for men, long or short blue or white dresses for women with maybe long or short veils. You can sometimes  tell which order a Sister or Brother belongs to—Franciscans, Dominicans, Benedictines, Redemptorists—by the kind of habits they wear.

Do you think habit is a funny word for clothing? Well, people who go horseback riding also sometimes wear a special outfit and that's called a "riding habit."

YOU probably use the word *habit* to describe something you do over and over again—like you are in the habit of brushing your teeth every morning or going to bed at the same time every night. So some Sisters and Brothers are in the habit of putting on a habit every morning!

When you grow up you may become an airline pilot, a soldier, a doctor, or have some kind of career where you wear a special uniform. What kind of uniform do you think it might be? Could it maybe be a habit?

**Do you have a sister or a friend or a mother named Mary?
Do you have a friend whose mother is named Mary?**

Sure you do. You have a friend and his name is Jesus. And his mother's name is **Mary**. When you have a friend, the friend's mother may be YOUR friend too. When you go to a friend's house to play, she may give you milk and cookies or a special treat. She may give you a hug or put a band-aid on your knee if you fall down and get an ouchie. She may listen to you if you have a problem or a long story to tell.

All mothers are special so Jesus' mother is especially special. That's why the Catholic Church calls her the **Blessed Mother** and honors her by putting statues or pictures of her in many churches.

Mary is not like God the Father or Jesus or the Holy Spirit. Mary is a friend's mother so you can say a prayer to ask Mary to ask her son to help you. You can say something like, "Please, Blessed Mother, tell God that I have a problem and I really really need help. Please, Blessed Mother, tell Jesus about my problem so he can tell me what to do about it." You can make up your own prayers or use one of the many Mary prayers the Catholic Church has put together—like the Hail Mary or the rosary.

Did you ever see someone in church holding a string of beads and praying? They're saying the rosary. Do you ever say a Hail Mary or a rosary to honor Mary or to ask for help? It's a merry good thing to do.

So what is a Hail Mary and what is a rosary?

Well, the **rosary** is NOT a bunch of roses, but it IS made up of a lot of **Hail Mary** prayers! You've probably seen a rosary— a string of beads plus a medal and a cross or crucifix. Some rosaries are very plain, made of knotted string. Some are very beautiful made of sparkling beads of bright colors. But every rosary is a reminder to help you think about parts of Jesus' life. These parts are called the **mysteries of the holy rosary**.

According to tradition, way back, hundreds of years ago, a priest named Dominic put strings of beads together to give to people so they could "finger" the beads as they prayed and that would help them keep their minds quiet and reverent instead of wandering around thinking of other things. Wasn't that a good idea?

Do you know how to say the Hail Mary or the rosary? If you would like to learn how, look in the little prayer section at the end of this book—OK?

And if you would like to learn about the rosary mysteries, see if you can find them somewhere else in this book!

When you look around your neighborhood, what do you see on the rooftops—a chimney, an antenna, a TV satellite dish or maybe at Christmastime, a plastic Santa Claus? Well, what do you see on a church roof?

Some churches have plain roofs with no decoration except maybe some lights at Christmastime. Other church roofs might have a **steeple** or a **belfry** or a **campanile**. You know *steep* means "something very high" and that's what a steeple is—a very high tower that sticks high in the air on the roof of the church so if you are looking for the church, you can see it from far away!

The belfry is high on the roof too, but it's called a belfry because it has big church bells in it—bells big enough to be heard several blocks away. Sometimes there are two belfries—one at each side of the church. Sometimes there is only one and when there is one alone it is called a campanile.

You might hear the big church bells ringing a few minutes before Mass to remind people that it's time to come into the church. The bells also sometimes ring before or after a funeral and at special times of the year. Sometimes—in a time of danger or a time of joy—all the church bells in all the churches in the city ring at one time.

Did you ever hear big church bells ringing from far away? What did they sound like—bong-bong or ding-dong? What did you think of when you heard them ringing? Did you like the way they sounded?

What should you do if you hear church bells ringing at noon?

No, the bell is NOT ringing to remind you to eat lunch! This bell usually reminds people to stop and say a prayer called the **Angelus**. *Angelus* is the Latin word for "angel" and this prayer reminds us of the time when an angel appeared to Mary to tell her she would be the mother of Jesus. Although most people only stop to pray when they hear the  bells at noon, it has long been a custom for some churches to ring bells at six o'clock in the morning AND at noon and at six o'clock in the evening. This reminds people to pray morning, noon, and night.

If you don't know the Angelus prayer, you can say any kind of prayer you like, but it is always a good idea to say SOME kind of prayer in the morning, and at noon, and at night.

Speaking of noon and lunch, do you know what you should do before every meal?

Yes, that's right—you should always wash your hands. But after that, what should you do? Catholics usually bow their heads and say a very short prayer to thank God for the food. This is sometimes called "**The Blessing**" and sometimes called **"Grace,"** and sometimes just "**Prayer Before Meals.**" You can make up any kind of blessing prayer but this is one that many people say:

> **Bless us, O Lord,**
> **and these your gifts,**
> **which we are about to receive**
> **from your bounty,**
> **through Christ, our Lord. Amen.**

Wondering about those rosary mysteries?

A mystery can mean a puzzle to be solved (like the mysteries in the *Nate the Great* or Nancy Drew books) OR a mystery can be a religious truth that can only be understood through faith. The rosary prayer is based on the "mysteries" of Jesus' life on earth.

Each **rosary** has five decades of ten beads (decade just means ten). As you say each decade, you think about a part of Jesus' life.

You start with the **Joyful Mysteries**: The Annunciation (when the angel announced to Mary that she would be Jesus' mother); The Visitation (when Mary went to visit her cousin, Elizabeth); The Nativity (when Jesus was born); The Presentation (when Mary and Joseph "presented" the baby Jesus at the Temple—sorta like when parents take their baby to be baptized today); and The Finding of the Child Jesus in the Temple (this happened when Jesus was about twelve years old and got separated from Mary and Joseph and they searched for him and found him in the Temple).

Did you ever hear any of those stories about Jesus? If you didn't, ask someone to tell you more about them—or look them up in a children's Bible.

The Joyful Mysteries were all about Jesus' life when he was a child. Can you guess which mysteries come next?

That's right. These are about Jesus' life as a grownup. They are called the **Luminous Mysteries,** or the **Mysteries of Light**. They are: The Baptism of Jesus in the Jordan (when Jesus was baptized in a RIVER!); The Wedding Feast at Cana (when Jesus performed his first miracle and changed water into wine); The Announcement of the Kingdom (when Jesus began going out to preach and teach the people how to live better lives); The Transfiguration (when three of Jesus' apostles saw Jesus mysteriously transformed and heard the voice of God speaking to Jesus); The Institution of the Eucharist (this was the Last Supper, the last meal Jesus shared with his friends, the apostles).

Yep, these stories are all found in the Bible too. You can look them up. Now see if you can find the other two series of mysteries later in this book!

**You can sing along, strum along, drum along,
trumpet along…and make a beautiful noise to the Lord!
But who does this and how?**

This is what the **choir**—and the people—do during Mass and
other Church rituals. The church choir is made up of people
who have nice voices and are happy to use them to sing and
praise the Lord. But all the people (including YOU) should sing
along with the choir because singing is like praying with music.
And you may have noticed that sometimes the choir sings along
with someone playing the organ or a guitar or maybe even a
drum or a trumpet!

Music is a very important part of the liturgy—and a very
joyful way to pray together.

Do you like listening to music? Do you like to play a
musical instrument? Do you like to sing in the bathtub or when
you're riding your bike or when nobody is listening? Would
you like to join a choir or just sing along with the others in the
congregation? Either way, you will be using the great gift of the
voice that God gave you.

Did you say, what is a congregation?

Well, that just means a group of people who congregate, who
come together to worship God, to get to know one another, to
help anyone who needs help, to share prayers, and to be like a
family or a community that are all friends of God.

Sometimes it's nice to be alone. Sometimes it's good to pray
alone. But sometimes it gets lonely alone and it's great to be a
part of a **congregation**! Aren't you glad you are part of one?

Ready for more rosary mysteries?

The next mysteries are about the sad things that happened on Good Friday so they are called the **Sorrowful Mysteries**. They start with The Agony in the Garden (when Jesus prayed and was then captured by the Roman soldiers); The Scourging at the Pillar (when the soldiers beat and hurt Jesus); The Crowning With Thorns (when Jesus was beaten after the soldiers placed a crown of twisted thorns on his head); The Carrying of the Cross (when Jesus was forced to carry a heavy cross to the top of a hill after he had been sentenced to death); The Crucifixion (when Jesus was nailed to the cross, suffered, and died to save the world).

Did you ever feel sad about something? Can you imagine how sad Jesus' friends must have felt? But they didn't have to stay sad very long. Do you know why?

After those sad mysteries, is there a happy ending?

You bet! That's why these are called the **Glorious Mysteries**!
The first one is called The Resurrection (when Jesus surprised
everyone by rising from the place they had left his body and
coming back to life!). After that, there are: The Ascension (when
Jesus' friends saw him rise or ascend into heaven); The Descent
of the Holy Spirit (when the Holy Spirit came down and
inspired the apostles); The Assumption of Mary (when Mary's
body was taken up into heaven); and The Crowning of Mary as
Queen of Heaven.

The mysteries begin with the angel telling Mary that Jesus is
coming and end with Mary rejoining her son, Jesus, in heaven.
Isn't that a happy ending?

Where would you see a T-shirt stained with ketchup? Where would you see blue jeans with grass stains on the knees? OK...now where would you see stained glass?

In LOTS of churches, you'll see **stained glass!** This does not mean the glass is dirty, stained with blueberry juice or a mud pie slushie. No, no, stained glass is very beautiful. It may be red like ketchup or green like grass, but it is made with a special process that stains, or colors, the glass in bright shades that shimmer when light shines through the glass. For hundreds of years, stained-glass windows have been used to decorate churches—and homes and other buildings.

Some churches do not have stained-glass windows but many do, especially the older churches and big cathedrals. The stained-glass windows are not just beautiful. The artists who make them sometimes put in pictures of Jesus, Mary, saints, or angels. And sometimes the pictures may also teach a lesson or be full of symbols.

Have you ever seen a stained-glass window? What pictures or symbols did you see in the window?

Now maybe you know what a symbol is—or maybe you don't. So what do you think a symbol is?

If you ever went to a professional baseball game, say the St. Louis Cardinals, you would see lots of pictures of a red bird named a cardinal—on hats and shirts and banners—because that bird is a **symbol** for that team.

When you see a flag flying in front of a school or carried in a parade, the flag is a symbol for your country. When you see two people shaking hands, the handshake is a symbol of friendship. When you see someone wearing a wedding ring, the ring is a symbol that reminds the person wearing it of the special promises made at the wedding.

Now what kind of church "symbols" do you think you might see in a stained-glass window in a church?

Do you think a church symbol might be a book or a candle or a loaf of bread or a bunch of grapes? How about a dove or a peacock or a pelican?

You might guess that a book would be a symbol for the **Bible** or a candle might be a symbol that Jesus is the "**light of the world**." You might guess **bread** and **grapes** symbolize the Eucharist since Jesus said, "This is my body and this is my blood" at the first Eucharist when he held up a piece of bread and a glass of wine made out of grapes.

But what about those birds? What do you think they are symbols for?

Look, up in the window...it's a bird, it's not a plane, it's a symbol!

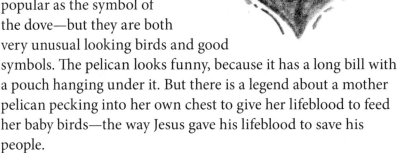

You probably guessed that a **dove** is a symbol for the Holy Spirit and a dove with an olive branch in his beak is a symbol for peace.

The **pelican** and **peacock** are not as popular as the symbol of the dove—but they are both very unusual looking birds and good symbols. The pelican looks funny, because it has a long bill with a pouch hanging under it. But there is a legend about a mother pelican pecking into her own chest to give her lifeblood to feed her baby birds—the way Jesus gave his lifeblood to save his people.

The peacock has a small head but a large fan-shaped tail of beautiful colorful feathers. When those feathers fall out, people save them to use for decorations. But each time a feather falls out, a new one comes in—and it's even more beautiful than the one before, the way Jesus died but rose to a more beautiful life. That's why the pelican and the peacock have both been used as symbols for Jesus' Resurrection.

Have you ever seen a pelican or a peacock at a zoo or an animal park? The next time you do, you can remember that they are special Church symbols.

If you would like to know about other Church symbols, see if you can find them later in this book...OK?

Did you ever see a seraphim in church?

You might have seen a statue or a picture of a **seraphim**, because seraphim is the fancy name for a kind of **angel**! These angels are supposed to have SIX wings—two to cover their face, two to cover their feet, and two to use for flying!

Do you ever get embarrassed and wish you had two wings to cover your face? Did you ever wade through a mud puddle and wish you had two wings to cover your feet? Did you ever wish you had two wings so you could fly? Wouldn't that be fun?

Are there any other kind of angels besides seraphim?

The word *angel* comes from a Greek word that means "messenger" and the Bible mentions angels several times—when they came to deliver messages. Two kinds have the best sounding names—the seraphim and the cherubim. Don't you like those names?

And there are also three **archangels**, which are maybe a little more important than regular angels.

On September 29, there's a special feast called Michaelmas, because it's the feast day of Michael the Archangel. But the two other archangels, Raphael and Gabriel, are also honored on that day. AND there's a wildflower called the Michaelmas daisy, because it usually blooms on or near that feast day.

Flowers are often named for special people—like the Pope John Paul II rose—but this may be the only flower named after an archangel!

If you had a chance to name a flower, who would you name it for—your best friend, your mom, your favorite saint, or maybe yourself!?

Which angel may be the most favorite?

Probably the most "popular" angel mentioned in the Bible is the **guardian angel**. It's believed that each person has his or her own special guardian angel who will watch over, guard, and guide them.

Isn't that a nice idea—that YOU could have your very own angel to always be with you and help you? What do you think your angel might look like?

Did you ever watch a parade—with marching bands and floats and lots of people passing by? Do you think you would ever see a parade in church?

You might! Except a church parade is called a **procession**. There are no marching bands, but sometimes there's music and sometimes everyone is singing. And there are lots of people passing by—priests and deacons and altar servers and sometimes a first Communion class or a Boy Scout or Girl Scout group or children carrying palms or banners.

And do you know who usually LEADS this procession? It's often an altar server (a young boy or girl) carrying the **processional cross**. This is a tall pole with a cross or crucifix on top—to show everyone that Jesus comes first.

On special "holy days," there is often a procession down the center aisle of church or maybe outside of the church or even down the streets of a neighborhood. In the procession, altar servers may also carry candles or banners and sometimes there may even be four men carrying a platform with a statue on top of it, decorated with flowers. So a procession really can be a little like a parade. Processions are a way to honor God in a special way on a special day.

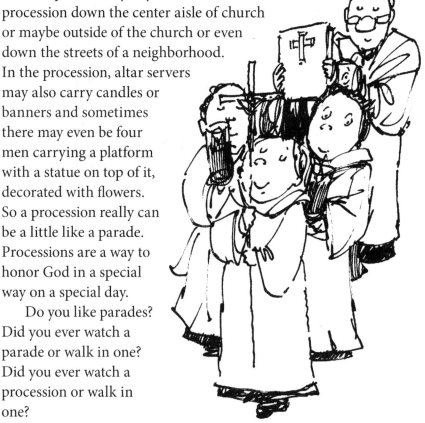

Do you like parades? Did you ever watch a parade or walk in one? Did you ever watch a procession or walk in one?

Sometimes in a procession you might even see a baldaccino. What could that be?

No, it has nothing to do with a bald man wearing a pair of chino pants. It's a very serious thing that you might call a canopy.

Have you ever seen a fancy bed that has four tall bedposts with a ruffly piece of fabric stretched across the top of them? That's called a canopy. Have you ever seen an airplane that has a see-through "bubble" over the cockpit so you can see the pilot sitting inside? That's also a canopy.

Those canopies protect the person in the bed or the pilot in the plane. In the same way, the **baldaccino** is a piece of fabric stretched over the top of four tall poles carried by four men or maybe four altar servers. It's held over a sacred object that is being carried in the procession—like the Blessed Sacrament in a monstrance—to protect it.

There is something else that is also called a baldaccino, and it's the "canopy" that is over a high altar in a church. If you ever go to Rome, Italy, you will see a very fancy baldaccino in St. Peter's Basilica that was designed by the famous artist Bernini way back in the Middle Ages.

There are probably not too many people you know who ever heard of a baldaccino. But now YOU'VE heard about it so you can tell them!

What kind of day do you think would be special enough to have a church procession?

The Church has all kinds of special days—like Christmas and Easter—and special seasons—like Lent and Advent—but they also have "**feast days**" that honor special saints or times that honor special people.

Can you think of a special day when your church had a procession?

What about Halloween or All Saints' Day?

You probably know that Halloween is actually the "hallowed" (or holy) "een" (or evening) before **All Saints' Day** (a feast day when we honor ALL of the saints) so many parishes invite children to come to church dressed as saints. They have a procession up to the altar and each child tells the story of the saint he or she is dressed as or explains WHY he or she WANTED to dress as that saint.

Did you ever dress up as a saint? Did you ever try to ACT like a saint? Well, why not?

What about a May procession?

The month of May is a special time to honor Mary, Jesus' mother, so many churches and schools have **May processions**. Since May is also the month when many flowers are blooming, children or adults bring flowers and walk in a procession to put the flowers near a statue of Mary. And one child or adult is chosen to "crown" the Blessed Mother.

A circle or crown is made of flowers and is placed on a statue of Mary, who is honored as the Queen of Heaven, and all those in the procession sing songs about Mary. One of the songs has the line, "Oh Mary, we crown thee with blossoms today, Queen of the Angels, Queen of the May."

Does your parish or school have a May procession? If they do, ask your family to take you to it. And if they DON'T, ask your pastor to please have one because it's a beautiful way to honor Mary in the same month when we all celebrate Mother's Day.

What other kinds of processions are there?

In some parishes, there are processions for special saints' days like **Saint Patrick's Day** or **Saint Joseph's Day**.

Saint Patrick was a bishop of Ireland so on his feast day, March 17, many people wear green or decorate with shamrocks or other Irish symbols and, in some cities, they have a big Saint Patrick's Day Parade or a neighborhood procession.

Saint Joseph is honored as the "breadwinner" for the **Holy Family** (the Holy Family is a name used for Jesus, Mary, and Joseph). So on Saint Joseph's Day, some parishes put up a table full of different breads and they decorate the church with flowers. After Mass, the people form a procession to go up and choose bread to take home to share with their families.

Saint Joseph's Day is March 19 so if your parish does not have a Saint Joseph celebration, ask your family to have some kind of special bread for dinner to honor the Holy Family's "breadwinner!"

Are you in a good humor today—or a bad humor? Whichever, did you ever hear of a humeral veil?

The **humeral veil** is another of those fancy words, but it simply means a very long scarf that the priest wears over his shoulders—during a procession. It's about eight- or nine-feet long and two- or three-feet wide and the priest uses the ends of the scarf to hold a sacred object he is carrying in the procession. He may also use this during benediction to hold the monstrance and make the Sign of the Cross with the monstrance.

Do you remember reading about the monstrance and benediction earlier in this book? If you don't, you can go back and look it up!

Did you know some priests wear things on their heads that have funny names too—a skullcap, cowl, or biretta?

Bishops and the pope (who are all priests) wear **skullcaps**, also known as a **zucchetto**, that are round circles that sit on top of the head—and are red for bishops and white for the pope. Some monks (who are priests) may wear a **cowl** that is attached to their long robes, much like the hood attached to your winter jacket. And lots of priests used to wear something called a **biretta**—but today you'd probably have to go to Rome to see a priest in a biretta. It's a square hat with three or four ridges on the side and a big pompom on the top.

Do you like to wear hats? Some people wear a skullcap with a propeller on top just for fun. Lots of folks wear hoods. But the only thing close to a biretta that you might see someone wear is that square hat worn by professors or students at a graduation ceremony. What kind of hat do YOU like best?

Now are you ready to hear more about church symbols? Do you think a fish or a lion or a snake could be a religious symbol?

You guessed it—they are! You probably know that a snake is often a symbol for evil or sinfulness and a lion stands for courage.

But the **fish** is one of the earliest Christian symbols.

After Jesus died, many people became Christians and followed his teachings. But the Roman soldiers were pagans who would arrest the Christians and throw them in jail. So the Christians had to start meeting in secret.

They chose the fish as a symbol of the early Church—a secret code—because the Greek letters that spell out the word *fish* also stand for the five words—Jesus, Christ, Son, God, Savior. To early Christians, the fish symbol stood for Jesus Christ, Son of God, Savior.

Luckily, the pagans also used the fish sign. They would leave the sign of a fish at a house where people would gather to share a funeral meal after a friend or relative had died. So the Christians would put a fish sign on one of their houses to tell other Christians to meet there that night for a prayer service. If the pagans saw that sign, they would just think they were having a funeral meal and they wouldn't come to arrest them.

Wasn't that a smart thing to do? Ever since then, the fish has been a special symbol for Jesus.

Did you and any of your friends ever have a club where you made up secret words or symbols for a code? Would you like to belong to a club like that? Well, you do! You belong to Jesus' Church!

What other symbols might you see in a church window?

You might see a boat or an **ark** (to remind you of the story of Noah and the Ark), a **harp** (for praise and worship), a **lamb** (one of many symbols for Jesus), a **crown** (for Christ the King), a **globe** with a cross on top (telling everyone that Christianity is taught all over the world), and, of course, a **cross** (in fact, many early churches were built in the SHAPE of a cross).

One of the reasons you see so many symbols in stained-glass windows and church art is because many long years ago when people started building churches, most people did not know how to read or write! Can you imagine? They could not read books about the Church or get online with a computer to learn about God so the Church used many symbols to teach them in a very simple way. The priests would explain to the people what the symbols meant and then, every time they saw a symbol, they would be reminded of the lesson it taught.

Aren't you glad you can go to school and learn how to read and write and use computers—and learn many "FUN-damental Facts" about God and his world and his Church?

Have you learned anything new about God this week? Has anything NEW or funny happened to you this week? Did you talk to God about it? Why not?

If your church does not have stained-glass windows, where might you see symbols?

Some time during the year, you may see some **banners** hanging on the walls of your church—and they will probably have some of the same symbols you would see in a stained-glass window. The banners also remind you of things. A banner might have a picture of the Bible or the Ten Commandments or a star like the Wise Men saw at Christmas or a butterfly or a pomegranate or a lion or an eagle!

The **butterfly** is a favorite symbol for Jesus because the butterfly seems to be dead when it is in that ugly shell called a chrysalis, but then it comes out all beautiful and full of new life the way Jesus came out of the tomb—all beautiful and full of new life.

The **pomegranate** is a strange fruit you may see in the produce section of the supermarket at Christmastime because some people make fancy recipes with it. It's about the size of a large orange and is reddish and if you cut into it, it breaks open and spills out lots and lots of pretty bright red seeds. This symbolizes the Church that is full of lots and lots of people and each of those people can go out and "plant a seed" by telling other people about Jesus and his Church.

Did you ever see a butterfly coming out of a chrysalis? Did you ever see a pomegranate or plant a seed? Aren't those interesting Church symbols?

When might you see lots of banners in church?

When it's time for a group of children to receive the sacrament of **confirmation**, each child sometimes makes a banner, using pictures of things that could be symbols for his or her family—and ALL of these banners are hung in church.

The children might use some church symbols mixed up with other kinds of things—a cross to show they are Catholics, a football to show they like sports, a fish to symbolize Jesus, a tree for the relatives in their family tree, a bicycle if they like to ride one, some stamps or rocks if they like to collect them.

Have you or any of your sisters or brothers received the sacrament of confirmation yet? If you wanted to make a banner—like a "coat of arms" or shield—to tell about your family, what symbols would YOU use?

Did you know you can pick a new name when you receive the sacrament of confirmation?

You don't have to, but many choose to give themselves a new **confirmation name** when they are confirmed and are "sealed with the gift of the Holy Spirit." The word *confirm* means to "give approval or strengthen or make sure of something," so this is a time to say OK to the fact that you were baptized as a Catholic and you now promise to live as a Christian. Since this is like a new beginning, many take the name of a saint that they would like to use as a role model.

What "new" name would you like to give yourself?

Now you know that confirmation is one of the seven sacraments. Do you know what the other six are?

First, there's **baptism**, the sacrament that you probably received when you were a baby. Then there's the sacrament of **reconciliation** when you go to **confession** and tell God, by telling the priest, what sins you may have committed and say you are sorry for them. Next comes the **Eucharist**, when you receive **Communion** at Mass. And **matrimony**, when people get married. And **holy orders**, when a man becomes a priest. And the **anointing,** or sacrament of the **sick**, which people receive when they are very sick.

As you get older, you may have some more questions about the **sacraments** so you should ask a relative or a teacher or a priest to explain them more fully to you. Will you do that?

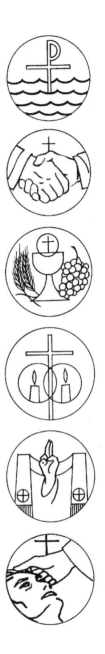

Now that you know the seven sacraments, do you know the Ten Commandments?

You have probably seen these listed in another book or in a children's Bible. The **commandments** are also called the **Decalogue** (because *deca* means "ten") and they are ten rules God gave Moses in the Old Testament as a way to lead a good life. They are:

1. I am the Lord, your God... you should not have other gods before me.
2. You should not take the name of God in vain.
3. Remember to keep holy the Sabbath.
4. Honor your father and your mother.
5. You should not kill.
6. You should not commit adultery.
7. You should not steal.
8. You should not bear false witness against your neighbor.
9. You should not covet your neighbor's house.
10. You should not covet your neighbor's wife.

Again, as you get older, you may want someone to explain these better (since right now, you probably don't own a house or have a wife!) but you CAN remember that word *Decalogue* and try it on some of your friends because maybe they won't know it just means the Ten Commandments.

You can find the commandments in the Bible—but do you know what the Bible is?

The word Bible comes from a Greek word that means "book" or a "collection of books" and there are LOTS of books—or chapters—in the **Bible**. Some of them have the funny kinds of names you might like: Exodus, Deuteronomy, Leviticus, Tobit, and Obadiah.

Although there are lots of "books" in this one book, Catholics think all the authors who wrote the words and stories in the Bible were "inspired" by God—so there is only one author. And who is that author? God!

You might like to listen to some of the stories from the Bible. They are VERY interesting.

What do you think a lion or an eagle have to do with the Bible?

Well, there are four books of the Bible called the gospels of Matthew, Mark, Luke, and John—and there is a symbol for each of those **gospel writers**. In the Old Testament, in the Book of Revelation, there is a line about "four creatures"—one with the face of a man and the others like a lion, ox, and eagle. Someone decided these would be good symbols for the four apostles who told about the "good news" of Jesus.

Matthew's Gospel tells about God with his family, so his symbol is a man with wings.

Mark's Gospel speaks of "the voice of one crying in the wilderness," so his symbol is a lion with wings since a lion lives in the wilderness but is also the king of the jungle the way Jesus is known as Christ the King.

The Gospel of Luke tells a lot about Jesus sacrificing his life by dying on the cross, so Luke's symbol is an ox with wings because many years ago, people (who didn't know about Jesus yet) would have a ceremony and sacrifice an ox.

And John's Gospel writes about Jesus being the Son of God the Father, so his symbol is an eagle, the bird that flies the highest and soars into the heavens.

Have you ever seen an eagle? It's very exciting to see an eagle soar high into the sky but you probably will never see a winged ox or a winged lion or a winged man—except maybe in a stained-glass window or on a church banner!

What do you think a groundhog would have to do with a blessed candle?

On February 2, the Church celebrates something called "**Candlemas Day**"—but February 2 is also the day we celebrate something called "Groundhog Day!"

Candlemas Day comes forty days after Christmas and is the feast of the **Presentation.** It celebrates the day when Mary and Joseph "presented" the baby Jesus at the altar of the temple (which was like a church) and offered two turtledoves because it was the custom at that time for parents to do that with a new baby.

At the Mass on Candlemas Day, the pastor blesses candles that people can take home so when there is a worry—like a big storm coming or someone who is very sick in the family—they can light the blessed candle and kneel down and say a prayer asking God for help.

That's why it's called Candlemas Day—but why isn't it called Turtledove Day instead of Groundhog Day? Well, there is an old legend that says, "For as the sun shines on Christmas Day, so far will the snow swirl in May..."—which means that if the sun is shining on February 2, it will still be snowing in May and spring will come late—but if the sun is NOT shining, then the snow will go away and spring will come early.

Then someone noticed a groundhog come out of his burrow on February 2 and the sun was shining so he cast a shadow and soon people began to watch for a groundhog on February 2 and if he cast a shadow, they would use this to forecast the weather!

Now on February 2, there is a big celebration in Pennsylvania when people gather to see if a groundhog named Punxsutawney Phil will come out of his burrow at a place called Gobbler's Knob. If he sees his shadow, it means bad weather to come and if he doesn't, it means sunny days ahead.

And that's the end of a very long story to explain what a groundhog has to do with a blessed candle.

Did you ever hear of a "poor box" in church?

In the past, most churches had a small box attached to a wall and it had a slit in the top where people could drop money to be given to help the poor. Today, instead of a **poor box**, churches usually have a basket or a container of some kind where people can put food or clothing for the poor.

And, since some poor people go to a church **rectory** (the place where the priest lives) to ask for meals when they are hungry, many churches have something called a "soup kitchen" where they cook and pass out soup or meals to anyone who comes asking for food. But did you know there's also a different kind of hungry?

When your tummy starts to growl, you might be hungry for a pizza or for a yummy home-cooked meal, but what do you do if your soul gets hungry? That's when some people go to church—to Mass—on Sunday or even on a weekday morning. They don't think it's just a duty or something they HAVE to do. They go to Mass because it's a chance to get closer to God, to pray, to "feed the soul" by receiving Jesus in holy Communion. Your body can't live very long without food and your soul needs to be fed too.

The next time you go to Mass, listen to the prayers and songs, and then talk to God during the private, quiet times. That's one way to make your spirit stronger, just like you make your body stronger by eating healthy food. Can you think of any other way to make your spirit stronger?

Do you sometimes wonder why people at Mass are always jumping up and down like they are in an exercise class?

They are NOT just jumping up and down—they stand, kneel, and sit at different times for different reasons. They stand to show reverence, kneel to pray, and sit to listen to the gospel and the homily.

And sometimes they also shake hands. Now at which **parts of the Mass** do you think they do these things?

You've already read about some things that happen at Mass—like the offertory, the lavabo, and so on—but how about all the other "parts" of the Mass?

This may seem kinda long, but it will explain at which times in the Mass people kneel, stand, or sit!

Mass begins with the **entrance** and everybody stands as the priest enters with the servers and often everyone sings an "entrance" hymn or song. Next comes the **greeting** from the priest and the **penitential rite** when the priest asks the people to think of any sins they have committed and then to pray together for pardon.

Next there is the **Kyrie** when people say, "Lord, have mercy. Christ, have mercy. Lord, have mercy." This is followed by the **Gloria**, the "Glory to God in the Highest" prayer, which can be said or sung. Then comes the **opening prayer,** which can change every day. And now it's time for the people to sit down and listen.

This is when you hear **reading I** and sometimes **reading II**, followed by the **responsorial psalm**, which again can be said or sung. And now it's time for the **Gospel**. Since this is very important, the people stand to hear this but then they sit down to listen to the priest's **homily**.

After the homily, the people stand again for the **profession of faith**—where Catholics recite what they believe: "We believe in one God, the Father almighty....We believe in one Lord Jesus Christ...."

By now, people have sung and prayed and listened to the readings and the homily and it is time for the **Liturgy of the Eucharist**, so the people sit down while the ushers take up an **offertory** collection and someone brings up the gifts and the priest prepares and blesses the gifts and then the people stand to pray over the gifts and to sing the **"Holy, Holy, Holy."**

It's time now to kneel because this is the most important part of Mass and during the **eucharistic prayer**, the priest says, as Jesus did, "This is my body....this is my blood..." and all the people profess their faith by saying or singing, "Amen."

If you've been paying attention, you may know that this is the time to stand and say the Lord's Prayer, the Our Father (if you don't know this prayer, you can find it near the end of this book).

Now it's time to make the **sign of peace** by shaking hands and/or saying "Peace be with you" to the people sitting near you.

To be ready to receive **Communion**, it's time to kneel and pray and be reverent before and after you receive the Body and Blood of Christ (or receive a blessing from the priest if you haven't made your first Communion yet).

After all have received Communion, you will stand for the **prayer after communion**, some parish announcements and the final **solemn blessing** of the priest. And sometimes you will sing a song at the end of Mass.

That's a lot to remember but now do you have an idea of when, which, and why people stand, kneel, sit, and shake hands at Mass?

During Mass, the priest and the people make the Sign of the Cross several times, but have you noticed when the people make this sign using their thumb?

When people stand for the reading of the gospel, look around and you will notice that many people use their right thumb to make the **sign of the cross** in three places—first on their head (to remind themselves to listen and learn), then on their lips (to promise to tell others about God's message), and then on their chest (to promise to keep this message in their hearts).

Did you ever notice that? It's a reverent thing to do—and it would be easy for YOU to do it, too!

The Mass is celebrated every day in many Catholic parishes, but there are also special "seasons" when there are different celebrations or services and you may see different colors or decorations in the church. Let's begin with the ones called Advent and Christmas.

Did you ever get tired of waiting—for your birthday or a trip to Grandma's or the last day of school? In the Catholic Church, the "waiting" time before Christmas is called **Advent**—and that's because *advent* means "coming" or "beginning."

Four Sundays before Christmas, the waiting starts—for the coming, the beginning. During this time, people pray and think about how wonderful it will be to celebrate Jesus' birthday. In some churches and in some homes, you might see an **Advent wreath**.

This is a circle of greenery with four candles

in it. The candles can be any color but usually there are three purple, or violet, candles and one that's pink. In church, the wreath may be hung from the ceiling. At home, it may be on the dining-room or kitchen table.

The first week you say a prayer, light the first purple candle and wait. The second week, you say a prayer, light two purple candles, and wait. The third week, you light two purple candles and the pink candle (for joy because Christmas is getting closer) and wait. The last week you light all four candles because Christmas will be here before another Sunday comes.

Did you ever see an Advent wreath in church or at your house? Did you ever have to wait a loooong time for something you wanted to happen? How did that feel?

After the Advent waiting, you will see lots of Christmas crèches. Do you know what a crèche is?

Crèche is an old French name that simply means "**manger**."
In the Bible story of the first Christmas, we hear that Mary
and Joseph had no place to stay but in a stable. So when Jesus
was born, Mary laid the baby Jesus in a manger, which is like
an open box where a farmer might put hay to feed the horses.
Today a crèche means more than just the manger—it's the whole
Christmas scene that you will see all over town, in front of homes
or buildings and always outside or inside a Catholic church.

Today's Christmas scenes include Mary and Joseph kneeling
by the manger where the baby Jesus is lying, but there may also
be shepherds and their sheep, a donkey, the Wise Men and their
camel, and maybe some angels. Sometimes there is an angel
hanging above the crèche with a sign that says, "*Gloria in Excelsis
Deo*" (Latin words that mean "Glory to God in the Highest!").

The crèche is a good reminder that Christmas is not just
asking Santa for toys or exchanging gifts with your family. Those
are wonderful fun and happy things, but we wouldn't have
them if Christmas wasn't Christ's birthday, a special holy day to
celebrate the fact that God sent his son to earth to save us.

Do you ever have a Christmas crèche under the Christmas
tree at your house or in your front yard? Do you ever go up to
look closely at the Christmas scene in church and maybe say a
little prayer?

What else might you see in church during the Christmas season?

You may see different kinds of banners and **decorations** and probably lots of big red flowers called poinsettias. These came from Mexico where they always bloomed at Christmastime and were called "flower of the Holy Night." They were first brought to America over a hundred years ago and now these bright red flowers are used everywhere for Christmas decorations just like white lilies are used for decorations at Easter.

You may also see a **Christmas tree** with blinking white lights. There are lots of stories about how a decorated tree became a popular part of Christmas, but one of them tells about a Paradise Tree. It seems that many years ago, churches would have a Christmas pageant or play where traveling actors or parish children would act out a Bible story. As part of this, they would sometimes have a Paradise Tree, which was decorated with apples, other fruits, and sweets. Children loved this and begged to have one of these trees at home. Later the sweets were replaced with bright lights to symbolize Jesus as the light of the world.

You probably have a Christmas tree at your home as well as at church. Would you also like to have a small **Paradise Tree** sometime?

Some families also have Advent traditions with straw and a cake. Can you guess what they are?

Some families put up the Christmas crèche with an EMPTY manger at the beginning of Advent. Every night, each child in the family can put one small piece of straw in the manger for each good deed he or she has done that day. If they do enough good deeds during Advent, there will be plenty of straw in the manger to make it a soft bed where they can put a statue of the baby Jesus on Christmas Eve.

Isn't that a good idea? But what about the cake?

Some families have a birthday cake for dessert and sing Happy Birthday to Jesus on Christmas Eve or Christmas day because it IS Jesus' birthday—the "reason for the season." Do you think your family would like to do that?

There are lots of **family traditions** and different ways to celebrate Advent and Christmas since this is such a special Church season. What tradition do you like best?

After Christmas, it's time for Epiphany.
Guess what that word means!

Again, **epiphany** comes from a Greek word that means "manifestation," which is another big word that means to "show" or "make known" (or show and tell!). This is celebrated in church on the Sunday nearest January 6, which is the feast of the **Magi**—or the three Wise Men who followed a star and came from afar to find the baby Jesus.

Do you know the names of the Wise Men? According to legend, there was Melchior who brought a gift of **gold**, Balthazar who brought **incense**, and Caspar who brought a gift of **myrrh**.

These may sound like very strange gifts to you, but they were the traditional gifts of HONOR in that time. They also symbolize the life of Jesus—gold for royalty, since he is Christ the King; incense (like we use in church today) for divinity, since he is the Son of God; and myrrh, which is a bitter herb and symbolizes Christ's suffering and death.

When the Wise Men came, the baby Jesus was first shown or manifested or "made known" to the world far away since the Wise Men traveled a long way to get back home and they told everyone along the way about the miracle of Jesus' birthday.

If you were going to visit the baby Jesus, what gift would you bring? A teddy bear, a tiny football, a musical toy? The best gift you can bring is your promise to try to be good, be happy, and always do the best you can—not just at Christmas, but all year 'round!

Did you ever hear of the twelve days of Christmas?

People love the Christmas season and want it to last as long as possible—and so does the Church—so they often keep Christmas decorations up and continue to celebrate in some way until after January 6. Those days between Christmas and the Epiphany are called "**The Twelve Days of Christmas.**"

Have you ever heard the Christmas carol that has that name? Did you ever sing Christmas carols? Some people go around the neighborhood, knocking on doors, and singing Christmas carols—another happy custom that celebrates the birth of the baby Jesus.

Have you noticed that when your family or friends have a new baby in the family, they can't wait to tell people about the birth and show the baby to everyone they know? They did that when YOU were born—and probably a lot of wise men and women came by to take a look at you! Maybe you cried a lot or maybe you smiled when they said "kitcheykoo" to you. What do you think Jesus did when the Wise Men came?

You've probably seen chalk in a classroom next to a blackboard, but what would chalk and a secret code have to do with the three Wise Men?

There's a very old Church tradition of **blessing your house** on or near the feast of the Epiphany. In years past, a priest sometimes came to the house with holy water and incense for this blessing but now a parent may do it—or anyone in the family. On or near January 6, the feast of the Epiphany, you go to your front door or main door and, with chalk, write a code on the door frame, then say a little prayer and maybe sprinkle the door with holy water.

So what is the code? Well, for the year 1995, you would have written 19+C+M+B+95. For the year 2006, it would be 20+C+M+B+06. Do you get it? For the year 2007, you would write 20 then the three letters and the 07 at the end. CMB stands for the names of the three Wise Men—Caspar, Melchior, and Balthasar.

AND those three letters also stand for the first three letters in the Latin prayer—*Christus mansionem benedicat*—which simply means "May Christ bless this house." And that's the prayer you can use when you put the chalk message on your door.

On the feast of the Epiphany, some churches will have small baskets near the church doors, full of pieces of chalk that has been blessed so you can take some chalk home for your blessing. But if your church doesn't have that, you can use any piece of chalk. And if people ask what that secret code means, you can tell them!

May Christ bless this house.

The next Church season is called Lent and it starts on Ash Wednesday. Did you ever hear of that?

During **Lent**, you will see lots of the color purple in church; on **Ash Wednesday**, you will see lots of ashes. If you go up to the altar, you will get a dab of ashes rubbed on your forehead in the sign of the cross and hear words such as "Remember, you are dust and to dust you will return" or "Turn from sin and be faithful to the gospel." This is to remind
you that Lent is a serious season to pray and think about the sad time when Jesus sacrificed his life on the cross on Good Friday.

The word *Lent* probably comes from a word meaning "springtime" since Lent always starts forty days before Easter. On the first day of Lent, people often decide to DO something for Lent as a sacrifice to show Jesus they appreciate the sacrifice he made for them.

Some think about WILL, others think about WON'T. Grownups might promise they WON'T eat junk food between meals or they WILL do an extra chore for a neighbor or the family once a week from Ash Wednesday until Easter.

Some children decide to "give up" something—like eating chocolate candy or watching one favorite TV show.

Others decide they WILL do something—like promise that from Ash Wednesday until Easter, they WILL help with the dishes every Thursday night or they WILL pick up toys in the family room EVERY night before they go to bed.

And during Lent, there is something else that Catholics do. As a remembrance of GOOD Friday, EVERY Friday during Lent—and on Ash Wednesday—they "give up" meat and eat fish or vegetables!

Did you ever get ashes rubbed on your forehead? Did you ever promise you won't or you will do something extra during Lent to show Jesus you love him?

So why does Lent start on a Wednesday?

Lent begins forty days before Easter and Easter is celebrated on the Sunday after the full moon following the vernal equinox. So that means Easter can come on a different Sunday each year and **Lent** always starts on Wednesday. Got that?

It sounds very complicated but Easter Sunday can come any time between March 22 and April 25 because it depends on when the **equinox** happens.

You may not have noticed it, but during the year sometimes the days are longer than the nights and sometimes the nights are longer than the days. BUT twice a year, when the sun crosses the equator, there's an equinox and the days and nights are EQUAL in length. One of those times is the vernal (which means spring) equinox. So after the spring equinox and the next full moon, Easter comes. And if you count back from Easter, leaving out the four Sundays of Lent, that makes Lent start on Wednesday. Got it???

However you figure it out, Lent lasts forty days to remind us of the story in the Bible when Jesus fasted forty days in the desert—and it helps us remember to "fast" from special foods or do good deeds for others.

What do you think would be the BEST thing for anyone to do or not do as a special way to tell Jesus thanks?

The Church calls the last week of Lent "Holy Week." Can you guess why?

That's right. This is the week with Holy Thursday, Good Friday, Holy Saturday, and the Easter Vigil. It begins with Palm Sunday and ends with the greatest holy day, Easter. It is indeed a **holy week**. So what will you see in church this week?

You will see lots of tropical palm branches, the priest washing someone's feet, darkness and light, the blessing of fire and candles and lots of white lilies. What a week!

Did you ever notice any of those things in church? Which ones do you remember most? Let's walk through this week and see what all happens!

You may see palms on a beach when you're on vacation, but what is Palm Sunday?

Do you remember the story of how Jesus rode into Jerusalem on a donkey and the people were so glad to see him, they waved palm branches to welcome him? People who travel to the Holy Land today can walk down the same streets in Jerusalem where Jesus walked when he was on earth and imagine how they would have felt on that day! It must have been like some parades in your town when people wave flags or banners.

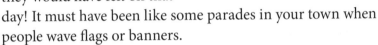

On **Palm Sunday**, the beginning of Holy Week, the priest blesses some palm branches and there is sometimes a procession of children or altar servers carrying palm branches down the center aisle to the altar. Sometimes there are palms at all the church doors so people can pick them up.

(And FYI, for your information, after Palm Sunday, leftover palms are burned and these are the ashes used on Ash Wednesday!)

In case you are wondering WHY palms, that's because palm trees and olive trees were the kind of trees that grew in Jerusalem, and it was the custom for people to wave those kinds of branches to honor someone. Today, if there are no palms available, willow branches, olive branches, or other kinds of greenery are blessed and used in the processions.

After this joyful reminder of Jesus riding into Jerusalem, the story of Jesus' passion (which means suffering) is read so this Sunday is also called Passion Sunday.

Would you like to go to Jerusalem some day and walk on the streets where Jesus walked?

Do you know why Holy Thursday is so special?

This day reminds us of the night Jesus and his apostles got together to have a nice meal, but it became a very special meal because when Jesus gave bread and wine to them, he said, "This is my body and this is my blood." This was the beginning of the Eucharist, the beginning of the priesthood. **Holy Thursday** is the time we especially remember Jesus and his apostles at the Last Supper, just as we do at every Mass when the priest says the words Jesus said.

After the Holy Thursday Mass, the priest puts the Eucharist, the Blessed Sacrament, into a monstrance and places it on a side altar of the church where there are usually flowers and candles. Then people just quietly leave the church BUT—during the night, people often come back to church to make a visit and honor Jesus in the Blessed Sacrament.

Did you and your family ever come back in the night to say a prayer in front of the monstrance on the side altar?

Wait a minute—something else happens at the Holy Thursday Mass. Do you remember what that is?

That's when you will see the **washing of feet**. The priest will actually wash people's feet!

Ahead of time, twelve people from the parish will be chosen to take the place of the twelve apostles—and in the middle of Mass, they will come up to the altar, sit down, and take off one shoe. With the help of the altar servers, who bring a pail of water and some towels, the priest will kneel down and go from person to person and wash their feet! This is a very old custom in the Church that recalls how Jesus was God but he was humble enough to wash the feet of his apostles.

Way back then, the apostles probably wore sandals and the roads were dirt roads so their feet were probably very dusty and maybe very tired so it must have felt good for Jesus to do that—but it must also have been a big surprise to the apostles.

Some very important people would never be humble enough to wash someone's feet—but Jesus was.

Did your mom or grandma ever take a cool cloth and wash your face and hands and then your hot dusty feet after you've been outside playing? Didn't it feel good?

When you grow up, would you like to be one of the twelve chosen to have the priest wash your feet like Jesus did?

Do you know why the day after Holy Thursday is called "Good" Friday?

Since this is the day Jesus was crucified, it might seem like it should be bad Friday but it is **GOOD Friday**, because Jesus died to save all his people—a very good thing. This is a quite serious day in church when people sometimes come and say the Stations of the Cross together or alone. There is no Mass this day, but there are several different services or devotions.

One of them is called the *Tre Ore*, Italian words that mean "three hours." In some parishes, people gather and pray for three hours, from noon until three in the afternoon, in honor of the three hours Jesus hung on the cross.

The main service is the Good Friday liturgy, which contains three parts. In the first part, someone reads from the Bible about the passion and death of Jesus. In the next part, a large cross is brought into church in a procession and placed at the front of church. While the choir or the people sing, each person in church goes up to the cross and either touches it or kisses it as a sign of sadness and sorrow for Jesus' death. After that, people receive holy Communion. Because there is no Mass, the hosts they receive were consecrated at the Mass on Holy Thursday.

On Good Friday, adults also "fast," which means they only eat two small meals and one regular meal but nothing in between. This too is to honor this special sad day.

Did you ever go to church on Good Friday and kiss the cross? When you say the rosary, you can kiss the crucifix on it. And if you have a cross on the wall at home, each time you pass it, you can touch or kiss it as a small way to honor Jesus. Would you like to do that?

After Good Friday, can you guess what comes next?

Yes, of course it's **Holy Saturday**. If you enter the church on Holy Saturday night, most of the lights will be out and you will get a small un-lit candle to take in with you.

Then you will sit quietly in the dark until the priest lights and blesses the Easter fire (sometimes in the parking lot, sometimes in the vestibule or back of church). From the flaming fire, he will light the very large Easter candle and then put out the fire.

From the light of the Easter candle, the altar servers and ushers will light smaller candles and then they will go through the church, lighting all the small candles that the people are holding until the whole church is alight with tiny glowing candles. Then the priest and servers will come down the center aisle in procession, stopping three times to hold up the Easter candle and sing, "The Light of Christ." All the people will answer by singing, "Thanks be to God."

This is called the **Easter Vigil** and it's a very joyful time when the altar is decorated with flowers and banners, holy water is blessed, people who have been studying to become Catholics are baptized, the choir and people sing Alleluia, bells ring out and all rejoice that Jesus Christ is risen from the dead!

When you go to the Easter vigil, you start out in darkness but by the time you leave, all the candles are lit, all the alleluias are sung, and you will feel like rejoicing that Jesus is the light of the world.

And you might want to go up and check out that Easter candle because it is VERY interesting.

So what is interesting about that big candle?

It's called the **paschal candle** and all during the fifty days of the Easter season—until Pentecost Sunday—you will see the light from this big candle on the altar. Then it will be taken to the baptistry, where it can be used to light the baptismal candle when there is a new baptism. So you won't see it on the altar again until another Easter comes. If you go up and take a close look at it, you will see it is decorated in a very special way.

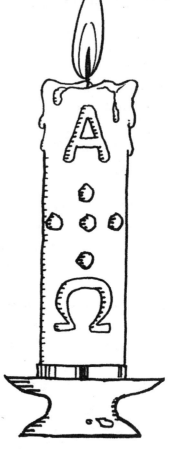

It usually has a cross cut into it and grains of incense are inserted into it with special red wax "nails" at the ends of the crossbars and in the middle of the cross. Some say these red marks remind them of Christ's blood. And some say this candle reminds them that Jesus is the light of the world and will remove all the darkness from your mind and heart.

But that's not all you will see on the candle. You will also see the year's date (like 2006 or 2007 or 2012) and the letters from the Greek alphabet—alpha and omega.

Do any of your friends speak Greek? If they don't, you can tell them that alpha and omega mean the same thing God is— "the beginning and the end."

After the Easter Vigil, it's time for a glorious Easter Sunday so how will you celebrate?

If you and your family don't go to the Easter vigil, you will probably go to Mass on **Easter Sunday**. And on the altar, you will see the paschal candle lighted and all the Easter lilies and decorations from the night before. And again, the choir and the people will sing Alleluia, which means "Praise the Lord."

Of course you know all about Easter eggs and new Easter clothes and Easter baskets—but all those customs or traditions came from the religious celebration of Easter as a joyful holiday.

Does your family have any special **customs** or **traditions**—like eating turkey on Thanksgiving Day or going to the opening game of the baseball season or singing songs in the car when you're going on vacation? Isn't it great that your family AND your church have so many happy traditions?

After Advent and Christmas, Lent and Easter, what do you call the rest of the Church year?

Would you believe that after those special seasons, the REST of the year is called **Ordinary Time**? Of course, there are still special feast days and celebrations, and besides, ordinary time can be special too—like the ordinary times in your life when you can just play with your friends, hang out with your family, or chase the dog around the yard.

Just remember that nothing about God and his Church is ordinary. Everything that God made is EXTRAORDINARY— like zebras and zinnias, wildebeests and wildflowers, mountains and moonlight—and YOU!

Now you've learned about symbols and seasons and sacraments, but do you know what sacramentals are?

These are very different from the seven sacraments, but they are also special things in the Church. They can be religious signs or symbols, special devotions or prayers or actions, types of music or objects or religious items that have received a special blessing.

Some **sacramentals** are used in public, in the church, like the holy oils that are blessed and used for baptisms, ordinations, blessing of the sick, or the blessed palms that you receive on Palm Sunday or holy water or candles or sacred songs.

Others are "things" that have been blessed by a priest, things you might use in private—like a medal you wear around your neck, a rosary, a small statue or picture of Saint Francis or the Blessed Mother you put somewhere at home.

If you ever shop in a sports store, you might see all kinds of things used in sports that you never noticed before. If you ever shop in a religious goods store, you might be surprised at all the "religious" things you never noticed before—like small holy water fonts, small statues, or different KINDS of religious books or prayer books or rosaries or crosses or scapulars or a medal with a picture of your favorite saint.

These are the kinds of things you might get when you make your first Communion. Do you have any of those things? Would you like to?

In addition to "things," what kind of sacramental "actions" have you seen or heard about?

There are many little **religious customs** or traditions like folding your hands when you pray, lighting a vigil light, dipping your hand in holy water when you enter the church, genuflecting before you enter the pew—things you may know about. And maybe there are some that you have just heard about.

Did you know that for many years—before you were born— it was the style for men and women to wear dress-up hats for special occasions—like when they went to church? It was the custom then for women and girls to always wear a fancy hat or a lace veil over their hair to go to Mass as a sign of respect since they were going into God's "house." And men often wore hats too—not a baseball cap or a stocking cap but nice felt hats called a fedora or maybe a derby. It was just the opposite custom for men who always took OFF their hats in church AND whenever a man passed a Catholic church, he would always tip his hat as a sign of respect, the same way he would dip his knee to genuflect in church.

These customs were not part of the Church's formal prayer, but they were "sacramental" or religious because the people did them to show that they honored and respected God.

In the same way, some people have a private little "altar" in their home—just a small table or shelf where they put a Bible or a small statue of a saint and maybe a flower or a candle. This gives them a place where they can sit or kneel and quietly say private prayers.

You might like to make a little "altar" of your own at home OR every time you pass a Catholic church, instead of tipping your hat, you might like to nod your head and say something like, "Hi, God, I love ya."

Did you ever hear of a saint named Blaise—and what would he have to do with a sacramental?

Saint Blaise's feast day is on February 3 and every year, on that day or on the Sunday closest to that day, people come to church to get the **Blessing of Throats**. They all stand in line and the priest or deacon will hold two blessed candles (which are sacramentals!) crossed under each person's throat and say, "Through the intercession of **Saint Blaise**, bishop and martyr, may the Lord free you from evils of the throat and from any other evil." So WHY do they do that?

According to spoken tradition, Saint Blaise was a bishop who was put in prison and then killed because he was a Christian. But while he was in prison, Saint Blaise cured a young boy who was choking to death with a fishbone in his throat. Everyone thought this was a miracle so they began to pray and ask Saint Blaise to ask God to help them when they had any kind of throat problems—and they would ask the priest for a "throat blessing." Eventually, it became a church custom to bless throats every year.

Did you ever stand in line to get your throat blessed? Did you ever hear the story of Saint Blaise and the fishbone? There are SO many interesting stories about Catholic saints—stories of adventure, courage, sacrifice, and mystery—from the saint who was kidnapped by pirates to the one who rode a donkey backward, from peasants to kings, from heroic priests to saintly housewives. Why don't you ask someone to get you a book about saints so you can hear more stories like the fishbone one?

Do you know what a patron saint is?

A "patron" is someone who would help you or protect you or maybe give you something without expecting anything back. A patron might pay your tuition at a special school or give money to help get a new roof for the church. So a patron saint is like that. Catholics do not pray to saints the way they pray to God, but they DO sometimes ask for their help—the way you might ask your mother to ask your father or ask Aunt Sue to ask your mother to give you permission to do something or go somewhere. Did you ever do that?

If you were named after a saint when you were baptized, this can be your **patron saint**. If not, maybe your parish is named after a saint and you might like to honor that saint. OR when you hear the stories of the saints, you could choose the one you like best to be your patron or "role model."

Would you like to have a patron saint?

Is there any special church prayer that mentions saints?

There are lots of prayers that people have put together through the years to honor saints and to ask the saints to pray to God for them but one special one is called the **Litany of the Saints**.

A litany can be a chant or cheer that's repeated over and over, like when the cheerleader at a football game shouts out the name of their team and that team's fans shout it back, over and over.

But a litany can also be a prayer that is repeated over and over. Saints are often mentioned in the liturgy and the Litany of the Saints is included in many devotions. On Holy Saturday, sometimes the choir SINGS this litany. They will sing the name of a single saint or a list of saints and the congregation will answer. For example, they will sing "Saint Joseph" and the people will sing, "Pray for us." Or they will sing, "Saint Ann, Saint Cyril, Saint Elizabeth, Saint John" and the people will sing back, "Pray for us."

Did you ever go to a football game or a baseball game and cheer for your favorite team by doing the wave or shouting the team's name over and over? Maybe some day you'll be in church when they have the Litany of the Saints and you can "cheer" for the saints, over and over!

The litany is a different kind of prayer and so is a novena. Do you know what that is?

The word *novena* simply means "nine," so a novena is a special prayer you say for a special intention BUT you say it EVERY day for nine days!

Do you think you could remember to do that? Why don't you try it some time?

Speaking of prayer, now that you know some of the answers to fundamental questions, how many fundamental prayers do you know?

You probably know some of them, but here are a few you might like to learn if you DON'T know them, OK?

Let's start with a special prayer for each day of the week.

SUNDAY would be a good day for Saint Francis' Peace Prayer.

Lord, make me an instrument of your peace. Where there is hatred, let me sow love. Where there is injury, pardon. Where there is doubt, faith. Where there is despair, hope. Where there is darkness, light, and where there is sadness, joy. Grant that I may not so much seek to be consoled as to console; to be understood, as to understand; to be loved as to love; for it is in giving that we receive, it is in pardoning that we are pardoned, and it is in dying that we are born to eternal life. Amen.

MONDAY starts the week so it would be a good day to use Saint Patrick's Prayer when he asked for

God's power to guide me,
God's might to uphold me,
God's wisdom to teach me,
God's eye to watch over me,
God's ear to hear me,
God's word to give me speech,
God's hand to guide me,
God's way to lie before me,
God's shield to shelter me,
God's host to secure me.
Amen.

TUESDAY would be a good day to say the popular prayer known as the OUR FATHER or the Lord's Prayer.

Our Father, who art in heaven, hallowed be thy name. Thy kingdom come, thy will be done on earth as it is in

heaven. Give us this day our daily bread; and forgive us
our trespasses as we forgive those who trespass against
us; and lead us not into temptation, but deliver us from
evil. Amen.

**WEDNESDAY is the peak of the week—a good day for you to
make up your very own prayer. What will you say?**

**THURSDAY would be a good time to say the HAIL MARY—
or to learn it if you don't know it now:**

Hail Mary, full of grace. The Lord is with thee. Blessed
art thou among women and blessed is the fruit of thy
womb, Jesus. Holy Mary, Mother of God, pray for us
sinners, now and at the hour of our death. Amen.

**FRIDAY is the day Jesus died so it is a day you might want to
learn this prayer and say it every Friday:**

The Act of Contrition

My God, I am so sorry for not being as good as I could
be, and I hate all my sins because I dread the loss of
heaven, but most of all because they offend you, my
God, who are all-good and deserving of all my love. I
firmly resolve, with the help of your grace, to confess
my sins, to do penance and to act better. Amen.
*(You can also say this prayer when you receive the
sacrament of reconciliation.)*

**SATURDAY already? A short prayer is good for a weekend
day so here's a good one:**

Serenity Prayer

Lord, God, grant me the serenity to accept the things I
cannot change; courage to change the things I can; and
the wisdom to know the difference. Amen.

How About the Rosary?

You read about it earlier in this book—but not how to say it.

First, make the Sign of the Cross while holding the crucifix in your hand. Then recite the prayer that tells you about most of the things Catholics believe. It's called the

Apostles' Creed

I believe in God, the Father almighty, creator of heaven and earth. I believe in Jesus Christ, his only Son, our Lord. He was conceived by the Holy Spirit and born of the Virgin Mary. He suffered under Pontius Pilate, was crucified, died, and was buried. He descended to the dead. On the third day he rose again. He ascended into heaven and is seated at the right hand of the Father. He will come again to judge the living and the dead. I believe in the Holy Spirit, the holy catholic church, the communion of saints, the forgiveness of sins, the resurrection of the body, and the life everlasting. Amen.

On the first bead, say an OUR FATHER. On the next three beads, say a HAIL MARY (to ask for faith, hope and charity).

Then say: Glory to the Father, and to the Son, and to the Holy Spirit, as it was in the beginning, is now, and ever shall be, world without end. Amen.

Think about the first mystery, then on the first big bead, say another Our Father. On each of the ten beads in each decade, say a HAIL MARY, then a GLORY TO THE FATHER...

Repeat this on each decade.

Think of the mystery, say an OUR FATHER, then ten HAIL MARYS, and a GLORY TO THE FATHER...

That's all there is to it. Since the rosary is such a long prayer, some people just say one decade at a time. Some families occasionally get together and say five decades for an evening prayer. And some people say the whole rosary every day.

Now that you've learned a lot of fundamental facts and fundamental prayers, what is your favorite fact or prayer?

Do you like the funny words like aspergillum or monstrance or thurible or do you like the stories behind the mysteries of the rosary or the names of the vestments?

Do you like the prayers that everyone says together or the private ones you make up on your own?

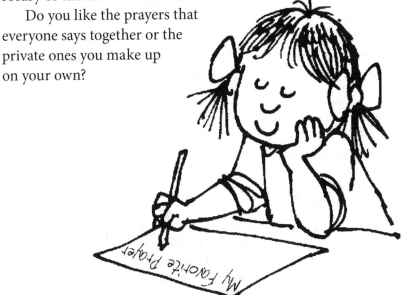

You've probably noticed that prayers usually end with the word *"Amen."* Now you have come to the amen part of this book...but...when is the end not the end?

Although this is the end of this book, there will never be an end to learning about all the wonders and mysteries and beauties and joys of God and his Catholic Church and Christianity. Hopefully, this book has answered SOME of your questions. But maybe today and surely as you grow older, you will have more questions. And that's normal and wonderful. The only way to grow and learn is to keep asking and seeking. But there is one thing you must remember: even though you cannot see or hear or touch God, you can FEEL him with you and you can KNOW he loves you—and there is **no end** to that!

Index